Differently Enabled Adventures

PUSHING THE LIMITS OF WHAT IS POSSIBLE

by Katrina Plato & Carrie Aadland

Peggy & Patrick,

Thank you for your warm hospitality and engaging conversations. It is always a delight to visit you both. I'd love another conversation after you have a chance to read this book.

With great affection,

Katrina

katrina@sensuousearth.art

Written and edited by
Katrina Plato
Contributing text by
Carrie Aadland

ISBN: 978-0-57870288-9

Proceeds from the sale of the book will go to two groups featured in the book: a wheelchair factory in Antigua Guatemala called Transitions: mobilizing Guatemalans with disabilities through rehabilitation, education, leadership skills, social integration and employment. And to the Rolling Pilot, Michael Glen, the first paraplegic hot air balloon pilot who now travels internationally to speak with youth about overcoming personal challenges to meet their life goals.

Table of Contents

Acknowledgment

We are grateful to the inspiring individuals we met during our 2019 adventures.

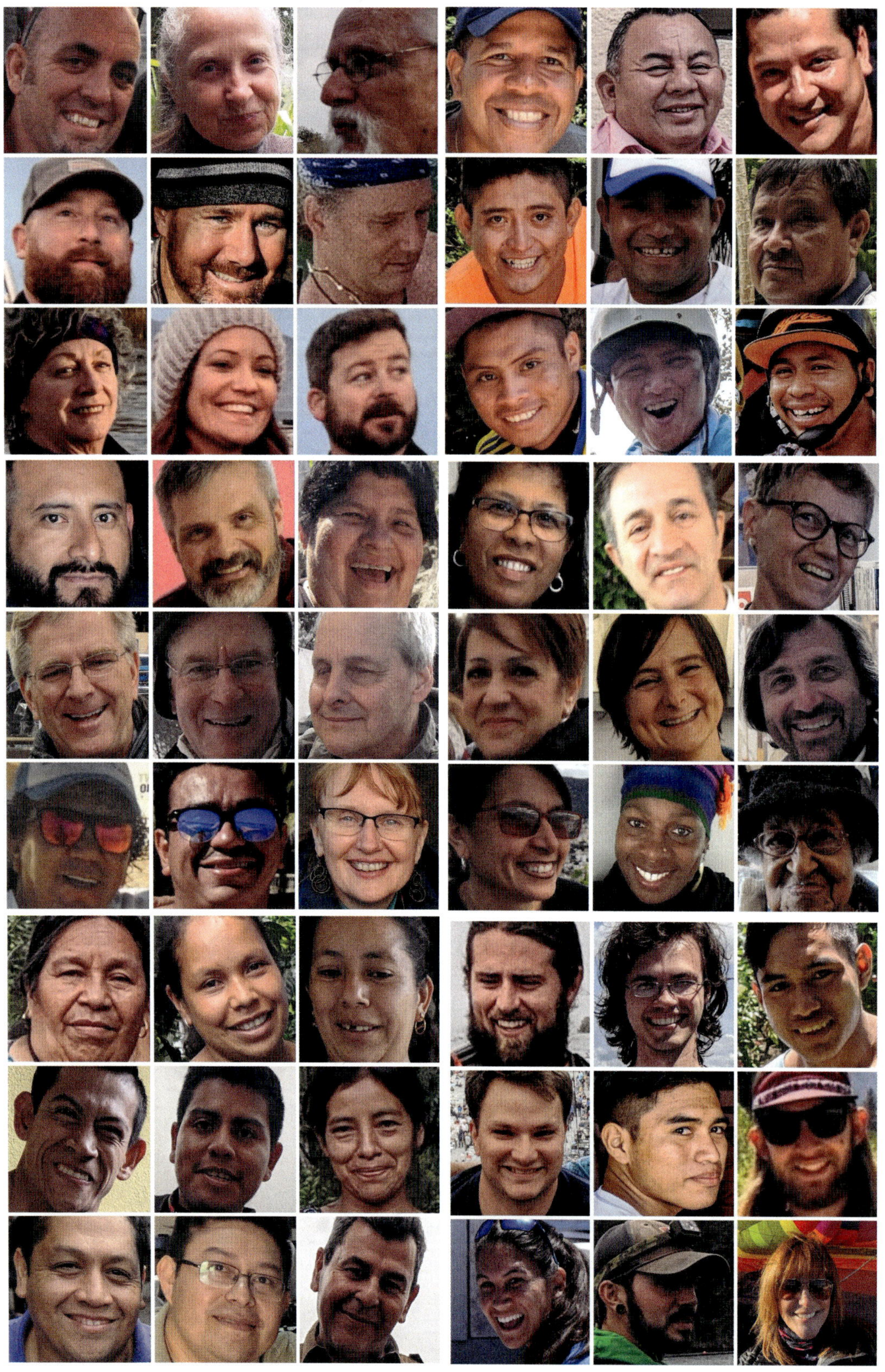

Foreword

"To travel is to live," is a popular quote. And today to travel overseas is a reachable dream for many. I live in Antigua, Guatemala, a relic of the colonial past of Central America. I am a street Guatemalan tour guide whom, as many guides in our beautiful town of Antigua, is someone who earns their living out on the streets of the Monument City by selling walking tours on the spot. Life is like a surprise box, or like "a box of chocolates," Forrest Gump would say. Every day we are out on the streets looking for tourists to guide.

I was in a corner of the main plaza of Antigua when I saw these two women coming down the sidewalk towards "my" corner. This was the first time I met Carrie Aadland and Katrina Plato. I offered them my services, which they politely declined but I helped them anyway to get Carrie and her wheelchair down to the cobblestone street from the sidewalk. Then I observed them go across the street and disappear among all the other people at the park... but they came back! I discovered then that they were not the average tourists I was used to dealing with. They were not interested in the stuff that normal tourists do. As a team, Carrie had piercing thoughts and seemed to be acquainted with the local politics, a very unusual behavior for a "gringa," and Katrina was an art lover, a "dilettante." As our friendship developed I learned they were traveling together to experience the world and its people. I also got to know that Carrie had been sharing with Guatemala her blessings she had been granted by the Fountain, helping many people without any personal interest or any ambition to obtain something in return. I took them to this beautiful overlook point above the city, where Carrie would not stop to amaze me with her piercing questions. I was thinking for days about one question that I had never heard asked before: "Is there any institution in the world that you admire, that you feel is worthy to exist?" They were extraordinary questions from an extraordinary woman. I was very lucky to have the answers for some of her uncommon questions!

Today, I feel glad and honored I got to know Carrie. I told my friends about her and her incredible adventures in a wheelchair. I hope that any reader of their book will have refreshing feelings about human nature and emotions. And may this book help persons to be motivated to help others. Might you (whomever is reading these humble lines) add a grain of your sand too! You never know when you can inspire somebody. We might think all the time that we are not doing enough to help others, but if millions of people offer a grain of sand, we will have a nice beach!

I don't like to close without mentioning Carrie's right hand woman; like Batman having his sidekick friend Robin, Carrie had Katrina who mastered the art of traveling and helping others too!

Hopefully the reading of these lines will be as exciting as traveling yourself to these incredible places where they had been spreading the passion for living, traveling and helping others.

Sharing their experiences with others is also part of the life journey of this incredible couple through incredible places, which in turn got them in contact with incredible people from around the world. Having not more much to say, I will leave you with the quintessence of their Voyager Journal.

Hugo Gutierrez, Guia General de Turismo
Travel Consultant
Antigua, Guatemala 24 de abril 2020

Introduction: Katrina Plato

How I came to contribute to this book. This book felt destined from the moment I agreed to travel as an "Adventure Specialist" for Carrie. I simply allowed the content to emerge. I bought a cheap hand size imitation leather book to log my observations, and purchased one for Carrie. One journal for each of us. On our first night together, we created a writing format that we followed most of the year. Every day we worked together, at least five days a week, on the road or at home, one of us suggesting a writing prompt inspired from the day's events. We took turns, swapping days. We set a time of 15 minutes of free writing on the topic of the prompt. Then we read aloud as much of our response as we wanted, the person who didn't offer the prompt going first. We were faithful to the process, even recording our prompts and responses into a recorder when we were on the road and writing was inconvenient.

I began a blog, carriemehome.org, to document our journeys for our friends to read, and those that we met in our travels. Gradually, the blog took shape as I wrote, and then Carrie added her reflections. While playing with the format of the blog, I was inspired to create a special section recounting the challenges of accessibility with Carrie's wheelchair and physical strength. I became fascinated with the cultural response to accessibility, as well as the wide variety of creative means of transportation we discovered. This section of the blog was also easy to keep up with while traveling. I posted photos or a short video and limited myself to two paragraphs capturing the essence of my observations. It felt manageable to write, and I hoped would be "accessible" for those glancing through the blog.

As our time of travel came to a close, I saw the structure of a book had emerged. Following the format of our writing prompts, I suggested we each write a note about accessibility. Instead of responding to a question, I suggested we allow photographs to be the inspiration for our writing. Every two pages begins with my observations and introduction to our adventure and continues with Carrie's perspective as a wheelchair user.

Why should you look at this book? Whether you have a disability or not, I hope this book inspires you to live your life to its fullest capacity. Our first week of travel Carrie posed a question that lived with me as we traveled. She wondered if people would exclaim, "Have you heard what Carrie and Katrina are doing now!?" It would be something unusual, yet make perfect sense if you knew the two of us. I am excited to share with you, the reader, what we discovered by the end of this short book.

Why these trips? Carrie determined the location for trips each month that are chronologically represented in the book. I requested that we focus on portions of our trips that highlighted the accessibility of the adventure. I also emphasized the trips that weren't planned, the surprises that came towards us as we naturally traveled in their direction. Our experience with the Rolling Pilot at the beginning of the year set a tone for what was possible when we remained open to the moment. In writing about these trips I tried to capture some of those precious chance encounters and adventures that were fun and life changing.

Introduction: Carrie Aadland

How I came to contribute to this book. Being a rather wimpy kid growing up, I found myself attracted at this point in my life to adventures that can be made accessible: like kayaking, ziplining, rafting, tubing, snorkeling, parasailing. However, MS has put me on a wheelchair for 22 years and I can't walk or put weight on my feet at all. Compensations include being strong and limber so I can transfer and maneuver around on my knees. I also can see out of only one eye, hear poorly, deal with an ileostomy, mostly liquid diet, take shots and need a lot of sleep. In spite of this, I forge ways around enough of these complications that I can keep it together for a week here and there of adventuring. Amazingly I was blessed by eight months of this adventuring in 2019. When the new year of 2019 arrived, I put together money and plans and found an available adventurer in Katrina. Katrina has been an ideal partner for our travels this year: she's physically strong and daring, savvy about how to do things, is friendly and assertive out in the world, advocates for pushing the limits of what I can do and is delightfully playful.

In December, when we were planning our 2019 adventures, we came up with a focus of water. For Katrina, water is sacred. For me, water is access to activity. Focusing on water led to the Bible verse that we've celebrated during all these months. The verse frames all this adventure as a gift and a privilege from God.

> Psalm 24:1-2 ESV: The earth is the Lord's, and all it contains, the world, and those who dwell in it. For He has founded it upon the seas and established it upon the rivers.

Why should you look at this book? We have had significant experiences that I feel are worth sharing, especially for our family, friends and acquaintances. It might be interesting to people we've had adventures with along the way. We are decent photographers and writers. We have a unique cultural angle especially in Hispanic countries. The book's topic is light and doesn't demand anything from the reader. It may itch the adventurer found in most all of us. Reading about ways I was able to do adventures beyond my apparent abilities hopefully will open up possibilities for others to find a way forward when the first answer is, "no, you can't."

Why these trips? Beside choosing our trips for **water-play potential,** I turn toward the Hispanic people whom God has put in my heart. In Mexico, I had friends to see (you will see Maria and her family on page 46) as well as to check out a new child sponsorship program there. I've traveled to Guatemala since 1981 and I'm always eager to visit children and their families that I've sponsored there over many years (especially Rudy on this trip page 100-101). While in Guatemala we visited a group of Mayan women and their new cistern project I helped with, page 108-109). Also I lived in DC for ten years before MS sent me back to Centralia where I live now; I had worked in ministries such as Bread for the World (You'll see me in their office on page 57.) and still maintain close ties.

January 2019
Road Trip

Watsu Massage Pool at Gray Bear Lodge: Katrina

The adventures with Carrie began in the rolling hills of Hohenwald, Tennessee. My friends Adam and Diann, founders of the retreat center Gray Bear Lodge, agreed to host us during their off season. I encouraged Carrie to experience Adam's Watsu massage before we began our January road trip across country. I'd been to the retreat center several times, but now with a new lens. Gray Bear's gravel roads and stone pathways were not equipped to accommodate wheelchairs, but they opened their hearts to the challenge. Nick, a massage therapist, put his big biceps to work pulling Carrie up the stairs of her accommodations at the Lotus Loft. He was the first to teach me how to easily navigate stairs. Nick pushed Carrie across the yard to the Watsu pool. (Watsu is a form of shiatsu massage that takes place in water.) Adam's soothing calm voice of assurance that all would be well was complemented by Diann's common sense wisdom. Like when at the entrance of the Watsu pool she calmly suggested that a screwdriver may be the best way to return the rubber tire to Carrie's wheelchair that had become dislodged while transporting Carrie across the stone and pebble Watsu greenhouse floor.

Watsu Massage Pool at Gray Bear Lodge: Carrie

Yes, hospitality was abundant at Katrina's friends' yoga center. I took right to my main event--the watsu massage. Imagine a cold January day in Tennessee. And then being wheeled into this sunroom with natural heat, lush plants and a womb temperature pool. I did my best to preserve the experience by snapping photos. I'd really like to bring that tropical room back to Centralia.

Cadillac Ranch on Route 66 in Amarillo, TX: Katrina

Our road trip included several stops on the old Route 66, including the Cadillac Ranch. I commented that we couldn't get through the only entrance, a cattle gate. In my memory, Carrie demanded I get her out of the car. She wheeled herself to the gate, where she popped off her chair and pulled her butt onto the rails. Seeing her determination, I collapsed her chair and fit it through the gate to greet her on the other side. Done! The wheels collected a lot of mud, easy to wash off in the end. The trip was worth getting a little dirty.

Cadillac Ranch on Route 66 in Amarillo, TX: Carrie

I often start these tourist stops trying not to inconvenience Katrina. I intend to do as much as I can myself and say "no" on things that would require much lifting or straining. But admittedly, I end up wanting everything, and Katrina delivers with generous (and able) willingness. You can see the Cadillacs far in the distance in the first photo. Katrina did push me clear out there. I got to do all the fun, even spray painting the Cadillacs, in spite of mobility limitations.

Boating on Lake Havasu, AZ: Katrina

Due to the hospitality of Don Grunzweig and Camille Smith, we were able to go boating during the annual Lake Havasu balloon festival. We arrived at the boat dock buzzing with wows of exciting news that against all odds, Carrie was going up in a balloon the next morning. Carrie had asked me how to create adventures in the face of resistance. "We don't plan," I answered. This edgy adventure found us. We would learn to let each adventure happen, like this happened. The practice was to be open to the adventure without expectations, without attachment. Have faith in a vision and be persistent while allowing and opening to what unfolds. Being fully engaged in the experience attracts the adventure.

Boating on Lake Havasu, AZ: Carrie

Here's my view of the speed boat ride under the balloons that Katrina described on the previous page. Don and Camille had known beforehand that I was in a wheelchair and they prepared and mobilized so that I could have a comfortable experience. It went well, and turned out to be easier than we thought. To get to the boat, they rolled my wheelchair down the boat ramp. The transfer from my chair to a seat in the boat was easy. And like everyone else, I can scooch around the boat without having to walk. An affirming start to our focus on water adventures this year.

Balloon Chariot in Lake Havasu, AZ: Katrina

I never get tired of relating the story of how Carrie ended up in Michael Glen's Duo Chariot at the Lake Havasu Balloon Festival. He was her knight in shining balloon who had the seat that enabled her to float above the world. On the festival grounds where they sold tickets for balloon rides we strolled past a man in overalls covered with colorful patches, one of which read, "Pilot." I felt possessed to ask him. "Can a person using a wheelchair go up in a balloon?" (People generally stand in the baskets but Carrie can't put weight on her feet.) The pilot bluntly confessed that he wouldn't take Carrie up in his balloon due to liability. After drilling him with questions, he told us about a paraplegic balloon pilot who had a special basket that fit himself and one more person. "Is he here?" I asked. The pilot pointed in the direction of a tent. He might be. After more inquiries we were introduced to Michael Glen. He would be glad to take Carrie up in his balloon the next morning. The word "Experimental" was in huge type on the bottom of the chariot seat foreshadowing much of our adventures to follow.

Balloon Chariot in Lake Havasu, AZ: Carrie

Balloons are pretty in the air, but I didn't really want to pay to go up in one. But, hey, we're here, let's find out how much. We found out it didn't matter how much; no ballooning unless you could stand. What?! Now I had to ride in a balloon. Katrina went into action, looking around for authoritative balloon people and initiating conversations about my woeful plight. One person led to another, and shortly we had a balloon ride scheduled the next morning. It would be with a paraplegic balloon pilot who sat in a special harness, and had room for two. Katrina and I both had turns. It was such a special ballooning experience that we were sky high and smiling for days.

Las Vegas, NV, Zipline: Katrina

Our road trip was one of the most unique ten days of my life, with one event flowing into another. When one door closed, we would find a new open. Like the Slotzilla zipline in Las Vegas. We had done a lot of research on the line, so it was a big bummer that Carrie couldn't go up in Slotzilla in the end, yet we smoothly transitioned to another event, a new adventure on another zipline, followed by a visit to an arctic bar made of ice. I was inspired to "Carrie" this flow forward through the year. I observed how i greeted the world without effort, naturally. I enjoyed meeting new people in each place we visited. I saw reflected back in the faces of those we dined with how inspired we all become on this adventure. Something was emerging for me, a new way of being. I noticed a shift from overtinking life, to experiencing life. My big takeaway was Carrie's comment to me that in having fun we got, "Extra points for being playful."

Rio Zipline, Las Vegas

Las Vegas, NV, Zipline: Carrie

We made Las Vegas our last road trip spot because I wanted to go on a special zipline there called Slotzilla. This zipline is special because it accepts people in wheelchairs. We arrived promptly for our time slot on Slotzilla and got our wristbands. All systems go. Except one last form to fill out and, oh no, it asks if you have an ostomy. I do. Because of how much I wanted to do Slot-Zilla, I got the manager and negotiated from every angle I could. But no way around that ostomy. Was I in tears, shut down, crushed? Maybe a nanosecond. Instead I looked the manager in the eye and asked, "What else can I do this afternoon that is like this?" She consulted with her co-workers and someone came up with "There's ziplining off the top of the Rio Casino." Really, wow. Katrina and her GPS driving skills got us to the Rio Casino before dark. As time was running out, Katrina even used her GPS for finding the way from the parking garage through the massive casino to where the zipline started. We arrived and were quickly guided to a seat like a ski lift and buckled in. And zip we went. We started atop a 50-story tower, and cascaded more than 800 feet reaching speeds to 33 miles per hour. And then the backward zip up to where we pushed off. Ziplining, check.

Cancun, Mexico

February 2019:

Leavenworth, WA

The Enthusiasm of Flight Attendants: Katrina

I wish I had taken more names of flight attendants and assistants that engaged in conversation with us as Carrie moved from one flying vessel to another. Attendants' faces conveyed genuine curiosity as they heard about Carrie's travel intentions. Most fun was when we met an Alaskan Airline attendant thrilled to meet Carrie after having heard of our travel blog from another attendant on our previous flight. It felt like the stewardesses were meeting a celebrity! One attendant shared her thought that Carrie's stories might give some people "a little push of encouragement."

I noticed that being with a wheelchair user gets one to the front of a line, like being the first on a plane, or whisked to the front of an immigration checkpoint. There were also the advantages of attendants helping us fill out customs forms. These moments were balanced with patiently waiting to be the last to get off the plane, at Carrie's request. Or driving through a snowstorm to show up hours before a flight in order to have time to check in bags, register for an aisle wheelchair, and be chaperoned to the flight in time to be that first person on the plane.

The Enthusiasm of Flight Attendants: Carrie

Flying the friendly skies. If you have a wheelchair, I recommend you travel in airplanes. Every flight I've taken in my wheelchair years has provided service beyond expectations. I enjoy every moment in the airport, from checking bags, to going through security, to finding elevators instead of escalators, waiting at the gate, and boarding the airplane on the narrow aisle chair. I love the flight also, take-offs and landings, as well as being curled up in my seat on the runway or in the air. In addition, when I'm with Katrina, she touts me (and deservingly us) as some kind of travel heroes—bringing smiles and interest from the flight attendants. I lap it up.

The Grand Royal Lagoon, Cancun: Katrina

Cancun was my first overseas adventure with Carrie. Assisting Carrie with her wheelchair, I became sensitive to inaccessible roads and walkways. In our travels of old cities I started asking, "What did disabled people do throughout history?" I heard the response that people didn't live as long then. That was an answer? "What about now?" The city was old and difficult to change, they said. I began to photograph the most common entrances, exits, paths and roadways of our travels. In Cancun, Carrie preferred the older and more intimate Grand Royal Lagoon to the big resorts because she was given a room with a close proximity to the swimming pool. Paths were quite narrow, with multiple levels. Carrie preferred staff to assist her, when they were available. She taught me to give others a chance to assist her with a glance that said, "Katrina, don't push me!"

The Grand Royal Lagoon, Cancun: Carrie

Katrina observed the many steps and narrow sidewalks when we arrived at our hotel in Cancun. I had stayed there before but didn't remember these wheelchair obstacles I had to work around. My more vivid memories were of the friendly volunteer pushers that came along and helped each time I got stuck. In my mind, if there are helpers, it's accessible. I see in the photo how narrow the sidewalks are. I gained a lot, really a lot, of accessibility when I changed from an 18" wide chair to a 16".

Cancun Carrie Jungle Boat Captain!: Katrina

Witnessing Carrie drive a boat was one of my most exhilarating moments of the year. I was surprised and then nervous that we had to drive our own boat to the jungle in order to snorkel. I'd never driven a boat. Once to the boat, Carrie boldly announced she would be driving the little speedboat. I had fun filming her shouting into the camera as she drove that after using a wheelchair for 20 years, and seeing herself as a "wimp" most of her childhood, and with MS most of her adulthood, that at 63 years old she was driving a boat through the Caribbean jungle, FAST!

Cancun Carrie Jungle Boat Captain!: Carrie

Yes, this little lady in the wheelchair is the one who throttled across the Caribbean, keeping up with the speedy guide boat. To be fair, Katrina was a good sport even though she would have preferred slowing down a bit. My instructions from the guide were easy: “Keep up with me.” That’s all the permission I needed to punch the boat to its highest speed. First we went though this jungle passage, and then out into the open Caribbean. The boat ride got us jazzed for the destination activity.

Snorkeling in the Caribbean: Katrina

We truly do not know what the day will bring. That's a good thing, Katrina. It's a good thing." Carrie said to me, noticing that I was beginning to flow with the spontaneous and unplanned. I like structure, a lot, but this year I kept relearning the lesson of staying in the moment. Like when I noted there were no seatbelts in the taxi on the way to the boat dock. Carrie made a sign of the cross, "This is our seatbelt."

The young man Carrie followed to the coral reef saw how fast she drove, so must have assumed that she also knew how to snorkel. She didn't stare out into the water for long. In she went.... Carrie said to me later with a spark in her eyes, "It is shocking to me what you can get away with in Mexico! They don't have as many regulations as we do in the States, and I didn't have trouble adjusting to driving this boat today."

Snorkeling in the Caribbean: Carrie

Our guide in the speedboat ahead of us stopped, and I pulled up alongside. He came to our boat which I assumed meant it was time to snorkel. Because I try to cooperate and not be extra trouble, I started putting on my never-before-used fins and mask. Then, Katrina and the guide got the "let's be polite and let the wheelchair lady go first" attitude. Over the edge of the boat I went, and I don't remember much after that. I came up sputtering and complaining about my mask, and Katrina came to my rescue and adjusted my mask. I got the hang of viewing and then, oh my, actual snorkeling amongst gorgeous fish in crystal clear waters. It was my single most magical moment of our adventure year. Katrina was also enchanted and went more places with the guide to see underwater sculptures after I had tired and headed back to the boat. The fish shown here from the aquarium we visited the next day give you an idea of what we saw through our snorkel masks.

Cleopatra Carrie: Katrina

The Jungle Tour in Cancun had no accessible wheelchair ramp down to their boat docks. When we arrived, a guard wheeled Carrie backwards down the steep bumpy paved boat ramp. After our water adventure, I spotted the stairs that most tourists took to enter the park. The men who worked at the docks jumped to lift Carrie to the top of the stairs leading to the street above where a taxi waited. It was the first of many times that I witnessed Carrie as Cleopatra.

Cleopatra Carrie: Carrie

One thing about Mexico, they may not have the Americans with Disabilities Act (ADA), but they have their own ADA spirit. Here's how it works: someone like me in a wheelchair shows up where there are (lots of) stairs. Then, seemingly from nowhere, four strong men show up. With smiles and ease, they glide the person in the wheelchair up or down the stairs. Gracias, Mexico, from this wheelchair user, for your kind customs.

Cancun Cenotes: Katrina

A cenote, or "sacred well" to the Mayan culture, is a natural pool commonly found in the Mexican Yucatán Peninsula and parts of the Caribbean. Cenotes were formed in limestone rocks over millennia as rainwater dissolved the calcite in the limestone until the ground collapsed exposing a pool below. Cenotes are usually filled with turquoise pools of water fed by underground streams and often include caves.

In Cancun, the Kantun-Chi Ecopark's white gravel pathways and stone walkways led to a variety of cenotes. We chose to go to the largest cenote in the park where Carrie could captain a kayak. Since our taxi driver, Jose, offered to push Carrie's wheelchair I opted to go barefoot. But when I saw the steep stairs I ran back to grab my shoes to help Jose manage the chair down the stairs. By the time I returned Jose and Carrie were at the cenote. I helped Jose navigate the last few stone steps to the water. By the end of the year I learned how to easily distribute the weight of the chair to hop Carrie up and down stairs. As intrigued as I was with puzzling the most efficient path through sand and stone, the highlight of the afternoon was witnessing Carrie's freedom of movement as she played on the turquoise water!

Cancun Cenotes: Carrie

Before Katrina and helper Jose had caught their breath, I found myself kayaking on an ancient mayan cenote. Wow, something I never imagined--neither the crystal clear pool, nor kayaking in it. Helper Jose plopped down in my wheelchair for the duration. Katrina delightedly joined me in exploring the cenote, climbing on my kayak for a while. After my life of getting driven around by others, I enjoyed taking Katrina for a boat ride two times in Cancun.

ATV Amazing Cancun Park: Katrina

To our knowledge, the ATV Amazing jungle park had never before accommodated a person with physical challenges. It was when Carrie started climbing up a ladder to the closest zipline that the manager of the park, Moises, decided to clear the six ziplines in the park of residents to give space for her request. Though Carrie can't put weight on her feet, she can crawl and so it was agreed that she would be given the choice to climb the steep ladders with the option to stop. She went all the way. The lead staff member, Michael Yodanis, suited Carrie with gear. Other crew members took turns traveling beside her on each line. As Carrie zipped down her first line, Michael turned to me with a smile bursting at the seams. With excitement in his voice, he shared that in his career as a coach, he encouraged people to let go of their fear. He wished others could witness Carrie embrace her adventure alongside her challenges. The twenty staff in the park knew of Carrie by the time she landed after the sixth zipline. It was her birthday, and so everyone ran to the base of the sand pit to greet Carrie and then pulled her to the nearby courtyard where they formed a circle around her to sing "Feliz Cumpleanos".

ATV Amazing Cancun Park: Carrie

I saw the fun-looking zipline at this park and discarded what I had said about "Zipline, check" after the Las Vegas zipline. Suddenly I wanted to do this one too. But the owner said "you don't walk, you don't zipline in my park." Not one to give up, I found this manager on duty. His name was Moises. Could he be persuaded to override and let me zipline? I started negotiations: "I can crawl up the stairs on my knee pads; I can hold on tight; I won't do anything unsafe." Moises hesitated. I continued, "Katrina is with me; I speak Spanish." By now, Moises had started talking to other staff and planning how it would work. Hooray! I ended up doing all six ziplines with Moises supervising a large contingent of the park's crew. At the end it was all smiles after a successful zipline by a wheelchair user. Often the accessibility challenge is getting people to take a chance on the ways we are differently enabled.

ATV Amazing Cancun Park: Michael

Michael was the most gregarious member of the elite crew at ATV AMAZING. He especially was energized by taking a special needs person on their ziplines. The supervisor in charge that day, Moises, delegated important tasks to him to facilitate my zipline experience. He wrote this delightful account of our zipline day from his perspective. His narrative fits the video perfectly. (Find that on YouTube under "Wheelchair user Ziplines in Cancun, Mex 2019")

In Michael's words (translated from Spanish), here is how it all happened:

At first it was a little difficult to understand that she could do it. But after the negotiation with the manager, Moises, we realized that she was eager to do so. We knew because her eyes shone with joy and it was like a challenge for her and doing that activity would mark her life forever more. When we found out it was her birthday it was like putting a light to the adventure. I personally took on the explanation of security measures and translation. We also had an elite team experienced in running our ziplines. It was our first time with people with leg problems and even more ATV Amazing is a recreational park of extreme activities. I can assure you that she is very brave and her desire to live and achieve her goals was the driving force behind making her birthday so special. It also left us a lesson for life "Never stop fighting for your your dreams; everything is possible if you persist." Thank you very much for giving us this great unforgettable experience. You will always be in the heart of ATV Amazing Park.

PS: She has been the one and only so she will be remembered as our best Zipline challenge.

Parasailing in Cancun: Katrina

This was the least edgy activity yet of the year, as Carrie put it. She transferred easily to the boat and the rigging, and up we went! I noticed staff members at each adventure seemed to expect I knew what to do with Carrie. I was more companion than specialist. Carrie explained that having an assistant and using clear language were important to accessing adventures. Organizations like the parasailing tour seemed more at ease when she brought an assistant. And, when registering for our adventures, Carrie told me to use the word, "transfer." She could easily transfer from her chair. But what did transfer mean? On this day, a seasoned staff member with leather brown skin greeted us at check-in and strolled with Carrie and me down a long wooden dock to a boat, where she hopped off her wheelchair onto a seat inside the boat. When it came time to fly, she scooted her bottom next to the harnesses which lay on a flat platform of green astroturf at the back of the boat. A yellow chute was spread out by the crew. As the boat sped faster into the wide expanse of blue water and sky, the yellow chute filled with air to reveal a huge smile. Professional cameras were aimed at us to capture our every smile of excitement as the smiling chute lifted us up, weightless over the Caribbean where we spotted huge sea turtles and stingrays below. Because she could stretch her legs flat, landing on her butt was a soft conclusion to our Cancun adventure. She completed her transfers with a hop off the side of the boat and back onto her chair.

Parasailing in Cancun: Carrie

Right, not much edginess to this parasail. We tried letting go to add a thrill factor. Little did we know that our next parasail, the following month in Mazatlan, Mexico, would shake us up much more.

Sledding in Leavenworth, WA: Katrina

In sharp contrast to the turquoise waters and warm sun of Cancun, Seattle was having record snowfall. Perfect for a our winter sledding plans. I had checked in with Carrie the day before we left. Did she feel up to traveling through the mountain passes to the winter wonderland in Leavenworth? At my question, her arms pulled tight against her thin body. She grabbed her bottle of Snapple tea for a quick sip, and then threw it forcefully into the basket of her scooter causing it to bounce in protest. Her piercing gaze suggested I rephrase my question. It was the big local event we had planned for that February while home in Washington. Though stuffy and nauseous, she was set on going. I learned that Carrie did better in action than staying at home. Once on the road, I found her enthusiasm contagious.

Sledding in Leavenworth, WA: Carrie

What are friends for? Sledding in the snow was on my desired adventure list. Sledding downhill, I can spin on my saucer alone. But uphill, it took friends Huck and Nadine to pull me back up. I learned of their true affection that day! (Nadine makes another appearance in our summer floating photos).

March 2019
Mazatlán

Parasailing in Mazatlán, Mexico: Katrina

We were tenacious in finding access to the beach through a maze of hotels for this parasail event. Thankfully the parasail crew waited, giving us a flight that took us to our edge. Parasailing with this company in Mazatlán was more engaging compared to our flight in Cancun. I felt vulnerable in every respect. I simply stood on the sand with strings connecting me to a deflated chute behind and a rope leading from the harness to a boat in the distant waters. As I saw the boat speed away the parachute shot up into the sky taking me with it into the cool air. The gusts of wind were louder and more forceful sitting in a simple harness as I was tugged through the sky without a rigging connecting me to Carrie. I felt very exposed in the vast sky up there. In contrast to my nervous flutters, Carrie had seemed calm and cool when she took off. She was shown how to contact the team through the walkie talkie, and instructed how to pull the cord to help the parachute drop back to the ground after the flight. I heard others like myself letting out gasps of awe from the beach as we witnessed the crew lifting Carrie into the air. Then minutes later the family under the umbrella behind me burst into applause when the experienced crew guided her back into a perfect landing onto her wheelchair.

Parasailing in Mazatlán, Mexico: Carrie

Headsets and instructions about pulling the proper cord to land got my rapt attention. Definitely more skillful participation demanded than on the previous happy face parasail.

The elegance of the crew landing me directly to my wheelchair was striking. Search Carrie Aadland on YouTube and the title: "Up, Up and Away! Parasailing wheelchair to wheelchair."

Yacht Adventure in Mazatlán, Mexico: Katrina

Carrie introduced me to one of her oldest friends, Maria Gomez from Tijuana. Carrie invited Maria and her daughter and grandchildren on a yacht adventure to Deer island. The family didn't dress for swimming, but almost everyone ended up in the water anyway! Carrie's desire to go snorkeling developed some twists and turns with a kayak, a water floaty and pirates. That's what can happen, I learned, when one is open to adventures in the moment!

Yacht Adventure in Mazatlán, Mexico: Carrie

Part way into our yacht trip, I decided I wanted to snorkel, which meant getting into the water. I got a backlash of "There's nothing to see snorkeling here," "Don't complicate things","It's too cold." I stubbornly went anyway. Part way down the ladder, I agreed, it was cold (being the Pacific Ocean) and I was feeling shaky. I expected to hear from Katrina "Good, I'll help you back up," Instead, I heard "Carrie, keep going, you're almost at the next step, just a little farther." Now, that's the challenge I like to hear from an adventure specialist!

Empowering Water Play in Mazatlán, Mexico: Katrina

Carrie decided to swim to the Isla de Venados (Deer Island). The water was chilly and the fish were few with no sparkles. Carrie became weary and wasn't confident she could swim back to the yacht. I saw some kayaks on shore. Leaving Carrie in shallow waters, I quickly swam to retrieve one. I found three islanders in the nearby shack. None of them knew a lick of English, and at this point my Spanish was muy poco. After my hand gestures towards Carrie and the yacht a dark burly man pulled a kayak into the water. I paddled the kayak to Carrie who hadn't moved. Her demeanor shifted radically once she was in the vessel from frigid victim to animated captain! I chose to swim back to the yacht. Being in water is soothing to me. Maybe this is why I created so many opportunities to swim that day. Sorry there is not enough space to tell you what I stole from the pirates.

Empowering Water Play in Mazatlán, Mexico: Carrie

This was Katrina's day of strong swimming—back and forth from yacht to shore keeping us supplied with kayaks and other water toys. At the end of this day is the only time I remember Katrina saying she was tired.

I delighted in seeing the kayaks Katrina drummed up for our use. Especially this day, when I was able to row around with dear friend Maria's grandchildren for their first kayak adventure.

Cenote Swimming: Katrina

The Hotel Playa Mazatlán has an elaborate system of pools designed out of someone's fantastic imagination. There were children pools, with deep areas for adults and theme park style pirate ships with slides and various fountains. Then a lap pool where adults gathered for lively afternoon aerobics or waterplay, and then the adult water park with waterfalls flowing over a bar located in a cave. It was here that I took several photos of Carrie in her lizard pose basking in the sun. Above the cave were four different sized hot tubs carved into the rock, all looking over the breathtaking beachfront. The trails to the hot tubs were very tiny pathways. But past the hot tubs, there was a little gate that was just barely wide enough for Carrie's wheelchair to pass. The trail beyond the gate led on to a bridge looking over a small zoo of turtles and then wound around a mountain of waterfalls to a cenote tucked in the far corner of the resort. It was here that we found the most adventurous cenote of our travels. Carrie had to pop off her wheelchair to scoot through at least one cave. The cenotes were realistically designed so that we had to swim through a cave in very cold turquoise water to reach a large pool. Nervous, I didn't go deep enough, and bonked my head the first time through. After practicing our underwater swimming, Carrie and I returned to meet the challenge again.

Cenote Swimming: Carrie

I´m glad our focus on water activities brought us to another cenote in Mazatlán. Instead of the 5000-year-old natural Cancun cenotes, we had a fabricated cenote at our Hotel Playa Mazatlán. The architects and stonemasons and water and plant people sure did their homework because it was every bit as awe inspiring and challenging as the "real" cenotes left from ancient Mayans. Our first visit we wanted to swim through a cave from one pool to another. I prepared to use my snorkeling mask because there wasn't much room for air in the cave tunnel. True to form, I was graciously allowed to go first. I came up sputtering and a bit panicked But seeing a relaxed Katrina floating in the pool, always gives me confidence. The destination pool was glorious, beyond words, but look at the pictures.

I wanted a second swim in our hotel cenote to go more elegantly through the tunnel and to be submerged in that amazing pool again. So Katrina and I, in one of our most extreme cases of making the inaccessible accessible, trekked again to the cenote entrance, I maintained consciousness swimming through this time. Lots of Hurrahs!

Beaches in Mazatlán, Mexico: Katrina

Our room at the Playa Mazatlán overlooked a loamy beach of sand where Carrie and I met the athletic Jorge Luis Retana, a young man from Guatemala who lost a leg and foot in a train accident as a boy. After I spotted him on the beach, Carrie prompted me to go ask him how he maneuvered over the beach with his wheelchair. Jorge was having a picnic with two friends. He shared that his sports wheelchair made it through the sand as well as Carrie's, with the help of a friend winding the chair playfully backwards. Inspired by our conversation, I spun Carrie out to the beach so she could hear about Jorge's other traveling adventures.

Beaches in Mazatlán, Mexico: Carrie

A little wheelchair camaraderie on the beach—one place I don't often see others on wheelchairs. Wheelchair people generally want what normal walkers want. In this case, it was being with friends in the warmest sand and near to the waves crashing on the beach. But getting there is not easily done in a chair, and so it's a treat. Even though we'd never met, Jorge and I talked animatedly about how fortunate it was to find ourselves on a beautiful Mazatlán beach that day. Katrina later put Jorge in contact with an athletic wheelchair factory in Guatemala which warmly invited Jorge into their fold.

April 2019
Italy

Accessibility to Rick Steves: Katrina

The foremost leader in traveling to Europe, Rick Steves, happens to live in Carrie's home state of Washington. In preparation for our trip to Italy, Carrie and I went to visit his travel center. When we arrived at the center I spotted Rick walking across the street. We inquired within if he was returning so Carrie might have an audience. The tour guides said it was a rare possibility. With patience and persistence we waited and in turn Carrie received a very good five minute conversation with Rick. He opened by explaining he had been in his office finishing the introduction to Art Simon's book. It was a small world moment as Carrie had been the accountant with Bread for the World when Art Simon was the director. Another coincidence was that Rick was on his way back to Guatemala, where we would be going in July. Carrie spoke to me of her dream to work with Rick on accessibility travels. Maybe synchronicity will bring them together again.

Accessibility to Rick Steves: Carrie

Don't believe my dog's innocent face on Katrina's page—he almost blew the whole thing for us. When Rick first came out, Goliath growled loudly and stopped just short of sinking teeth into Rick's arm.

Rick Steve's vast array of European tours are not open to people using wheelchairs. He observes, "The creaky, cobblestoned Old World has long had a reputation for poor accessibility." However, accessibility is getting better and he refers travelers with mobility challenges to a company that leads specialized tours in Europe.

Rick Steves is a big deal in a lot of my circles and I left sky high on planning how to use, "I was talking to Rick Steves about that..." A couple of months later in Washington DC I got my chance. Here I am in the aforementioned former workplace, Bread for the World with current director David Beckmann. Small world, David had gone to Guatemala with Rick last November, and he also knows Rick through Rick's Bread for the World involvement. To top it off, for some reason the computer screen in the bottom photo shows Rick and I engaged in the conversation we were having on the opposite page.

Cobblestones In Rome: Katrina

Cobblestone is defined as, "a small, round stone of a kind formerly used to cover road surfaces". Whoever wrote "formerly" must not travel. In Rome the ancient pavers were a new challenge to navigate with a wheelchair. They look beautiful to my eye. But these roads made of stone took extra muscle. Even cars had to go relatively slow over the unpredictable terrain. In Rome the backroads were also smaller, which made the cars seem faster. I was full of questions. How have people with disabilities navigated these streets over the centuries? I felt almost giddy with the task of finding the easiest routes alongside cars and motorcycles, while hopping on and off the very inaccessible sidewalks.

Cobblestones In Rome: Carrie

Here, here to Katrina's dexterity in finding the fastest and most comfortable way through the streets of Rome. Katrina reminded me to point out instances in our travels when being in a wheelchair was not a detriment, but actually an advantage. It was on that afternoon in Rome. Traffic stopped for us and people along the way stepped aside, opened doors, and pulled me up steps. Katrina's excellence plus the wheelchair friendly Italians meant that we were able to view much more than I was used to seeing in a day. We practically "did" Rome in one afternoon, including a stroll along the Tiber River, listening to a street singer belting out opera, shopping for funky boots and eating gelato. And all that before we made it to the amazing Pantheon (which comes up next). As to cobblestones, I appreciate Katrina's efforts to ameliorate cobblestone discomfort. But I confess, as the rider, those in Rome didn't bother me a bit. But I acknowledged that the world's most perilous cobblestones awaited still in Guatemala.

The Pantheon In Rome: Katrina

The prize of our wandering over cobblestones was finding the Pantheon. A woman on the airport shuttle highly recommended the Roman monument. Learning that it was just blocks from our hotel, we set out for the historic temple. The next day I met a man while waiting in line to see the Pope who had also just visited the Pantheon. There were three things we found in common with our visit. 1. We had no preconceived idea what we would find. 2. We were in awe. 3. Once inside we did not want to leave. As the man and I spoke we noticed that we were both having a physical reaction in the telling of our stories. My body was warming up as I reconnected to the space. Not much is known about the temple. A circle in the roof is a window to the elements such as the rain, snow and sun. In my story, when the sun shines in this temple it reveals the sacred geometry within the womb of the Divine Feminine. I want to kiss the architect.

The Pantheon In Rome: Carrie

It was after 5pm when we came across the Pantheon, but it was still open with a long line waiting to get in. I was spotted by the guards and immediately a chain was taken down and we were ushered inside. The marble floors inside were as easy to glide my wheelchair on as a Costco warehouse floor, in spite of being 1893 years older. Katrina wasn't looking at the floors. I looked up to see a mystical glow around her as if in an altered state of adoration. I did share her amazement when we saw together the crescent moon in daylight through the curious architectural hole in the Pantheon ceiling.

In The Front Row to See the Pope at St. Peter's Cathedral: Katrina

Even our tour guide looked surprised when Carrie and I were whisked away by the Swiss Guard to a special section of the square to hear Pope Francis address the people that morning. Carrie was the very front chair facing the Pope. We were excited about this special treatment, until it began to rain. While many in the back of the square left, we had strict orders to remain in our seats. The handsome security guards passed out large yellow and white umbrellas, but still, everyone left soaked through.

In The Front Row to See the Pope at St. Peter's Cathedral: Carrie

Yes, the giddiness of being in the special "pope row" eroded in the pouring rain. No rain problem for Pope Francis. He came up in his enclosed popemobile and sat under a heated canopy. During that long wait for his Popeship I remember that Katrina was hushing me and nixing my suggestions to liven things up. She was also afraid I would do something Lutheran like yelling, "Those Indulgences were wrong." (I found out at the Vatican that day that those nasty indulgences helped finance Michelangelo's Sistine Chapel. It's complicated.) Overall, I admit it was Holy to be in a special aisle for people who couldn't walk and were put near the Pope in hopes that we would receive miraculous healing by the man who millions still believe is Jesus' direct representative on earth.

Painting Accessible in Rome: Katrina

Thanks to the trip advisory company, Viator, Carrie found a "Paint for Fun" activity on the back streets of Rome. After the tour of Barbara Medori's quaint studio she gave an introduction to our painting project. We were to create a small reproduction of an Italian classic. Carrie quickly turned to me demanding that I paint her canvas for her. Instead, I encouraged her to work on that one small area, the brown right there. I have witnessed Carrie as a brave spark when faced with physical trials. A severe inner critic occasionally blocks her artistic adventures. I was able to tease out her innate gift for coloring until she found her "on" switch as a novice painter. Creativity can be accessible to all, one space and color at a time.

Painting Accessible in Rome: Carrie

I was eager for this paint workshop because I loved seeing Katrina's artistic skills during this year. Even when she is spray-painting Cadillacs it turns out beautifully. And I was hoping that what Katrina would paint would end up on my walls at home as a special remembrance of the trip. What I didn't expect was that I would be painting also, and with this whimsical artist hovering over me. But Katrina eased my panic suggesting I see the painting project as a coloring book with lines and sections to color in. So, I painted too. Our session ended before the paintings were finished, but that's how it is with the masters; the paintings often have parts undone.

Accessible Tour of Pompeii and Herculaneum with Dario: Katrina

We found a raving review on Tripadvisor for an accessible tour of Pompeii and Herculaneum with a strong recommendation to hire a professional archeologist. Dario was worth every euro. We learned he gives free accessible tours one Sunday a month. We found that Herculaneum (seen at the top of the page) had more accessible paths than Pompeii, whose ancient roads of huge boulders were really difficult in a wheelchair.

Accessible Tour of Pompeii and Herculaneum with Dario: Carrie

Touring Pompeii, our second Italy event in heavy rain, I was crabby. I don't like to be wet in a wheelchair. However, looking at this photo on the left, I see a gorgeous archeologist with a big red umbrella, my pink rain pants, two rain coats and boots I had just bought in Rome. Time to stop complaining and appreciate how well I have it in my wheelchair on paved paths compared to the folks 2000 years ago in Pompeii. Pompeii in its day was hardly accessible with its uneven stone streets and steep stairs. But like in so many places, I left grateful for the ramps and paved trails that have been put in since then, and for the nice people who got me and my wheelchair through even where there were not accessible paths. And the best part, our archaeologist has invited us back to be his guest in one of the museums or archaeological sites of our choice in the area. Italy anyone?

The Amalfi Coast, Italy: Katrina

Carrie requested stopping along the Amalfi Coast to experience at least one of the small towns during our long winding drive (between our hotel in Sorrento and the tile studio in Luci D'Artista before Salerno). I wanted to get the drive over with, to get past all the near scrapes with tour buses around the tight turns. But in the end I was grateful for the pause, to take in the beautiful houses and places of worship hanging off the coastal cliffs. However, even the pauses were moments prone to adventure. Do you see the glint in Carrie's eyes? I never knew what to expect. What is she going to try now? I found myself negotiating ways out of what I perceived were dangerous moments, saying, "I don't think that will be in your best interest." But when I followed this strong willed woman, I often found myself exclaiming, "Wow! This was really fun!" We had chance encounters and saw magical places because of Carrie's tenacious spirit.

The Amalfi Coast, Italy: Carrie

But Katrina, the glint just happens. My mind machinates possibilities for more adventure. “I bet I could stick my feet in some water, or ask that guy to go out in his boat, or go freelance down a ramp.” In this case I’m on a concrete wall, pallets resting at my feet, some orange boat fenders, coarse rocks and the sea a very short distance. What to try first?

Good sense ruled out any attempt to have Katrina dragging a wheelchair through the sand and rocks just to splash in the Tyrrhenian Sea. This is the body of water which borders the Amalfi in the Province of Salerno of southern Italy.

We did however end up in a chique little Italian dress store, and brought home a treasure in this aquamarine bag that Katrina is holding in the photo. After the Carribean and now Italy, aquamarine was becoming a favorite color of our trips.

Amalfi Bathrooms: Katrina

Overall, I found Italy to be a very accessible country to wheelchair users. So I was surprised to find this very inaccessible public bathroom during our stop on the Amalfi Coast. It was a tight, small bathroom for those that could access it, at the bottom of the stairs, through a thin turnstyle and short hallway. I went across the street to ask the owner of a bar if Carrie could use their services. The gentleman didn't hesitate, graciously showing Carrie a much more accessible room.

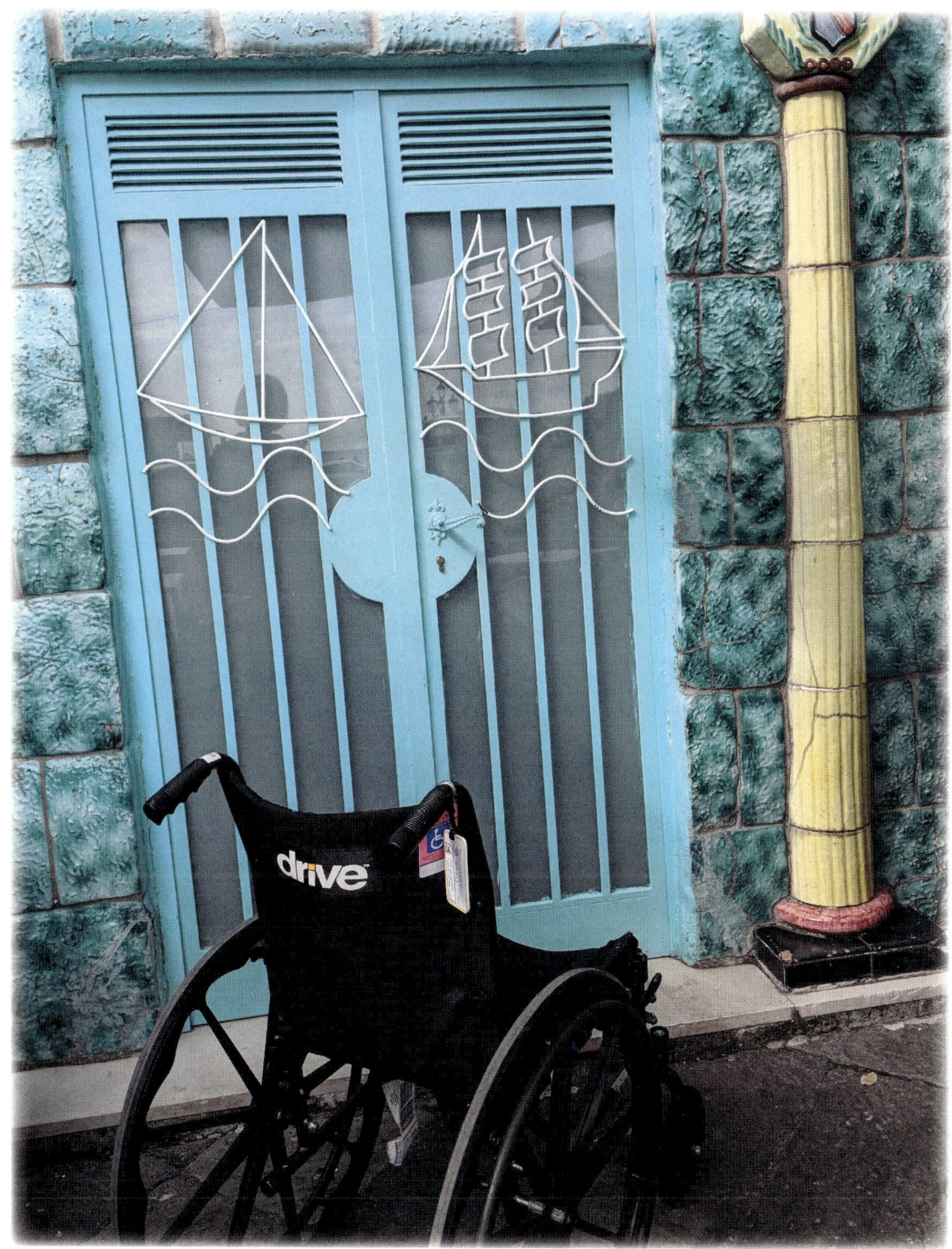

Amalfi Bathrooms: Carrie

Aha. Sometimes it's better to be the disabled one. I rubbed it in with Katrina after her experience at the dismal public bathroom. Mine was aquamarine with nice grillwork.

Now back to the car to finish the scenic drive along the stunning Amalfi Coast. And for another chorus from Katrina of "We're going to die, we're going to die!"

Palm Sunday in Mara, Italy : Katrina

Still recovering from the harrowing curves on the Amalfi coast, I was reluctant to drive the windy country roads from our respite at the Pianeta Maratea Resort to the little village of Mara. However, I'm grateful Carrie insisted. Our hosts at the resort said we were sure to find a Palm Sunday service in the village at the bottom of the hill. Carrie had noted that Italians were not quick to help her, while Mexicans often jumped to lift her chair. How much was that due to her fluency in Spanish and familiarity with the culture, I wondered? On this Palm Sunday the Italians may have made an exception in her case.The small church was packed, but the elders ushered Carrie to sit halfway up the aisle directly in front of the young dynamic priest. As her companion, I knelt behind Carrie's chair so parishioners could see the service. I couldn't understand the language, but was often brought to tears as I witnessed the community. I observed that women were leading parts of the liturgy. The choir kept their simple winter jackets on as they sang a cappella. All ages packed the chapel. As people turned to give hugs of peace I noticed many smiling faces looked weathered as if from sun and wind. As I gazed at the statue of Mary directly over the priest's head I felt a similar powerful presence of the Divine Feminine I had sensed in the Pantheon.

Palm Sunday in Mara, Italy : Carrie

A very serendipitous Palm Sunday church service in this Italian village. We drove around a corner seeking we weren't sure what, and came upon a Palm Sunday procession outside this church. We pulled over and were warmly welcomed. Someone gave us their parking spot so we could move out of the road. And others whisked me up a side ramp to the front doors and into the center aisle of the service in progress. Sometimes God's church gets it so right.

Cristo Redentore in Maratea, Italy : Katrina

I reserved the Pianeta Maratea Resort because of its view of the Cristo Redentore overlooking the Tyrrhenian Sea, an appropriate location for Palm Sunday. We arrived in the middle of the night with the Cristo lit as a shining beacon. The resort was deserted except for the hosts. Carrie and I were the only ones in the huge dining room for breakfast. We were two of maybe six people in the resort of over a hundred deserted rooms and a hollow olympic size pool. I found the lifeless concrete building unsettling. The head of housekeeping took pity on me and created my very own "office," providing a desk and chair in a vacant ballroom with vast windows overlooking the Cristo. Here I wrote on the blog about our travels. Carrie and I had a tearful meeting in this office as we watched the sun set. We learned the next morning that Notre Dame had been burning in the night. Might we have picked up on this emotional calamity? Our tour of Italy had several such significantly intuitive moments. As a respite from the empty resort I often visited the Cristo. It felt refreshing to walk past goat farms and ancient stone chapels to this beacon on the hill. I became grateful of the quiet. I learned tourists would begin to fill the countryside the following week for Easter. It took some coaxing, but I convinced Carrie it was worth a closer look to drive up and visit the Cristo before we left the quiet mountain.

Cristo Redentore in Maratea, Italy : Carrie

I was told that getting up to see the Cristo Redentor statue wasn't accessible. I was delighted however to see the stairs. I'm very comfortable getting to places on my knees. On my knees, I didn't see the actual statue until I reached the step I'm on in the photo. It made for a holy vista. Many times I'm warned that something is not accessible. If I try anyway, I often find an alternate, and sometimes wonderful, way to experience things.

Six Hours in Paris, with Air France: Katrina

It was a beautiful day in Paris, at the airport. France is known for their thinking, but in my opinion, they overthought their accessibility plan. With Air France, instead of going to the plane, the plane practically comes to you. I have never, ever, in my short life as a travel companion seen as much detail given to the care of individuals in wheelchairs as with Air France. We had to wait hours upon hours for the special tram that drove Carrie and a few others traveling a very short distance from the terminal to the entrance of their departing plane.

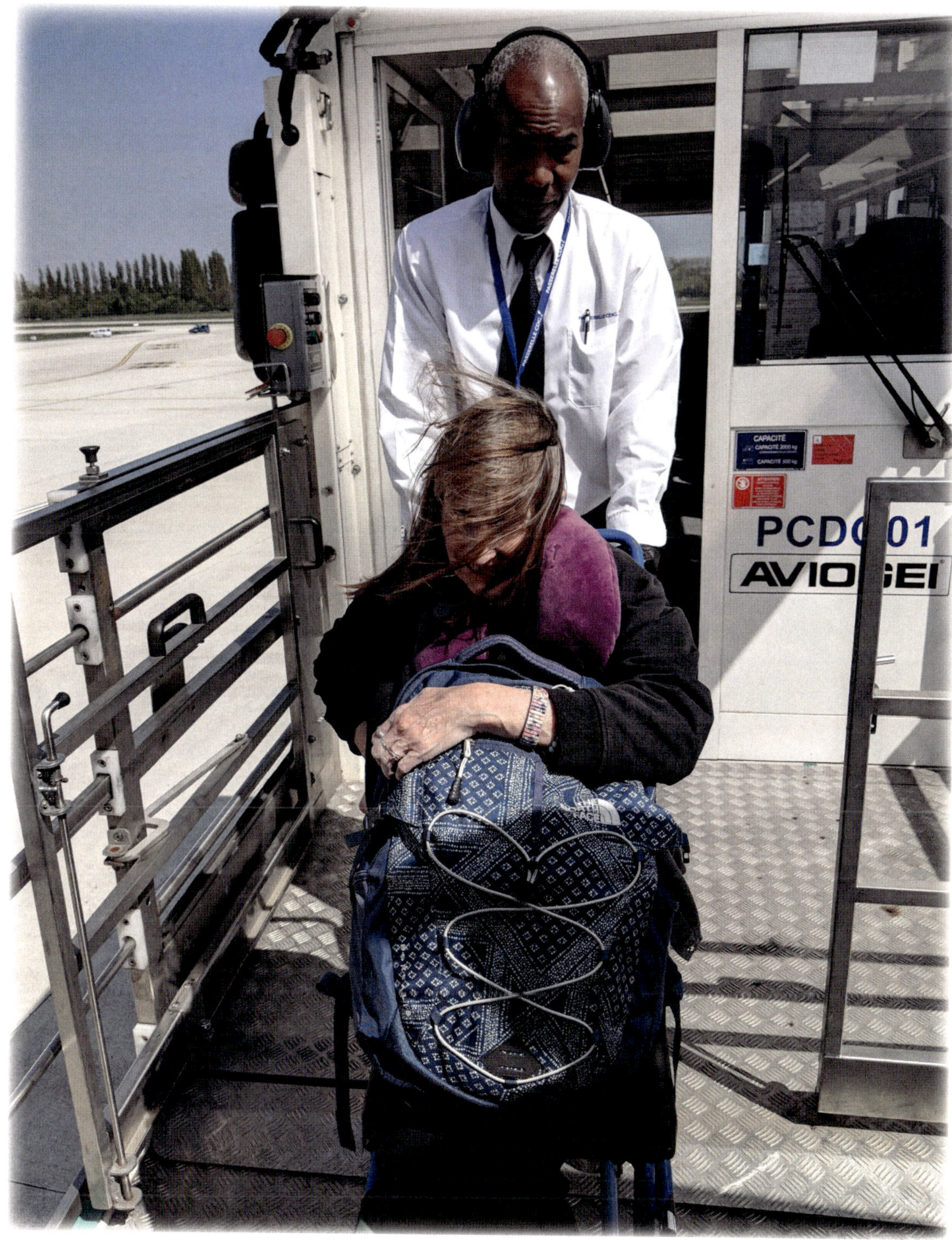

Six Hours in Paris, with Air France: Carrie

Tres Bien—six hours in Paris! Visit the Eiffel Tower? Talk Impressionism at a sidewalk cafe? Stroll the The Avenue des Champs-Élysées? It wasn't to be. Six hours was just barely enough time for the shenanigans of getting me and my wheelchair from one plane to another. It didn't take much longer than that to put out the fire in the Notre Dame cathedral (which was very much in the news after burning a few days before). So this is my Paris photo—with another concerned employee of the De Gaulle airport accessibility system.

May 2019
Washington, DC

Swinging by the Anacostia River in Washington, DC: Katrina

Swinging, a movement flying free brings back memories of childhood. While in DC, Carrie and I took several strolls to the wharf where we went to kayak, and to swing. Carrie would transfer her light body to the long wooden seat, and then used her body weight to gain momentum and height in the swing.

Swinging by the Anacostia River in Washington, DC: Carrie

These are big people swings. I went back time and again because all the swinging power comes from things I'm still capable of doing. Realistically, though, I'm not as independent on the swings as I like the pictures to show. Off camera, Katrina has to get me to the swing in the wheel-chair and return with the wheelchair when I've tired. Another of my tricks to look independent is to ask Katrina to move the wheelchair out of sight for photos. Katrina's other behind-the-scenes roles kept us able to do fun things that make good pictures. She was frequently on the phone finding out if something was open, what hours, and what the disabled access entailed. She did all the hard work of finding directions nearly every block of the way. Katrina's telephone and travel skills got us on many more fun adventures than otherwise would have been possible. You can see in our photos all we did in just one week in Washington DC.

Kayaking on the Potomac in Washington, DC: Katrina

In the course of our travels I began to notice a consistent pattern within myself. Though I was the "adventure specialist," I typically felt uncomfortable upon arrival in a new environment and hotel. But immediately after I got outside and explored the area I found miracles and synchronicities like: Route 66 Cafe across the street from our hotel in Rome, and now, the kayaking within a five minute stroll of Watergate Hotel. After a long day of travel, Carrie often preferred to get active once we got settled in our hotel. My pattern of discomfort was probably because I was tired of pushing and lifting and navigating. But each time she insisted, like this occasion, I was grateful for Carrie's spirit of adventure that said we immediately go outside the walls of the hotel and explore. This time we found an open dock along the Potomac with kayaks. The stairs to the dock did not deter her.

Kayaking on the Potomac in Washington, DC: Carrie

We rented the kayaks with no time to spare; they were closing soon. Good thing we pushed. A rainstorm that night closed the Potomac to all boating for the rest of our stay in Washington DC. My special needs dissipated in that kayak, clipping along with the very familiar DC skyline in the distance. Clipping along until I fairly quickly got tired. And as usual, Katrina had my back. In a kayak, this means that Katrina sits in the rear and paddles strongly when I falter. And a playful moment: Katrina did a double take when she saw this enormous plank I pulled out of the water.

Watergate Hotel Art Studio: Katrina

I was discouraged by the rain in May while in DC until a friend reminded me to access my skills to create an art studio in the hotel. The rainy days in DC became an opportunity. I set up the art studio on our huge windowsill overlooking the Potomac. The setting of natural light and a large flat surface felt ideal. After a visit to the gift shop in the National Gallery of Art for additional supplies, Carrie and I spent many quiet moments each morning or evening playing with colors while overlooking the swelling Potomac.

Watergate Hotel Art Studio: Carrie

Washington DC hotels are expensive, much more than even Rome. So why not stay in the Watergate?! It was fabulous, over and over. Even more so for a wheelchair user. The pool and jacuzzi were dreamy, so many ways to get in. Salt water so everyone can swim. An even dreamier changing room—elegantly stacked plush towels, wall dispensers for shampoo and such, and a swim-suit spinner. Our room had this million dollar view, perfect for being creative in Katrina's art space.

Rock Creek Park Labyrinth in Washington, DC: Katrina

Another perk staying at the Watergate Hotel was being just a few minutes stroll from a park complete with a labyrinth. The first time I spotted it, joggers appeared to be using the center as a meeting place before their run. When I entered the labyrinth, the joggers left. One by one people of all ages and colors joined me. A young nine-year-old girl hopped off her bike and ran the labyrinth. Then an older black couple slowly entered together for their first time. Then a young man parted from his sceptical friend who looked on as he also started the path. I was excited when Carrie joined me one afternoon. I don't know if she had ever been inside a labyrinth before. It was one of the rare labyrinths I'd seen wide and flat enough for wheelchair users.

Rock Creek Park Labyrinth in Washington, DC: Carrie

Katrina taught me about labyrinths. They are not the same as mazes in my puzzle books. They don't have dead-ends, and are deeper and richer. She invited me to do this outdoor labyrinth with her. It was meditative and I was prompted just enough to appreciate what I was doing. Then, I had another opportunity for a lesson in labyrinths. Coincidentally, the Watergate had a labyrinth inside the hotel. It was quite different in that it was made of thousands of pricey whiskey bottles. But it was equally as wheelchair accessible.

June 2019
Home on the Water and McCartney Concert

Osprey Rafting Co

Beach Wheelchair in Long Beach, WA: Katrina

I learned that the small town of Long Beach, Washington purchased three beach chairs for children and adult wheelchair users so they could have easier access to the beach. One of the chairs is kept at The World Kite Museum in Long Beach. The chair looks like a museum display, but once checked out, the chains come down and the chair comes to life with little effort. The kid in me leapt out with this light, easy to push chair. I made several short video commercials cheerfully pointing out the chair's accessible features while jerking Carrie back and forth in the toy as she maintained the role of the adult, calmly flying her peace kite. Visit the blog carriemehome.org to see my fun Beach Wheelchair advertisement or search Katrina Plato on YouTube and the title: "Beach Wheelchair."

Beach Wheelchair in Long Beach, WA: Carrie

We had a blast at Long Beach. The World Kite Museum there has these beach wheelchairs for use. I did have to get over worrying about people around gawking at this ostentatious chair and such an ordinary person in it. But with Katrina at the helm playfully pushing me around, things lightened up. Also add kite flying to your list of accessible beach activities. My peace kite took to the air in a blink and obeyed my commands with the string to dip and soar. Could Long Beach be more fun because of being in a wheelchair rather than being “normal’? The answer is written all over Katrina’s beaming face.

Osprey Rafting in Leavenworth, WA: Katrina

In May we began our summer rafting adventures on the Wenatchee River. I had never gone rafting, and would probably still be dry if it weren't for Carrie's desire to go floating this summer. Carrie and I started with a calm class one float in May, just the two of us with our young guide, Owen on flat waters. I witnessed that Owen had an ease with the river and a similar confidence with Carrie as he encouraged her participation in the water. Next was a splashy class three rapids in June with a full boat (seen on Carrie's page), and Owen again as our guide. Floating is very different than rafting, we learned. In July I kayaked through swirling rapids while Carrie enjoyed floating the river in a tube. The June splashy class three rapids were my favorite.

Osprey Rafting Co

Osprey Rafting in Leavenworth, WA: Carrie

I never thought I'd be doing this. I'm naturally wimpy with obvious accessibility issues. But, with Katrina along and the kindness of young guides at Osprey Rafting, here I am bouncing through class three rapids. At one point in our whitewater rafting trip, everyone had to get out of the river to walk around a dam. Not me, I got portaged alone in one of these big rafts. It took eight strong people to carry the raft overland with me in it. I kept thinking of Sacagawea having to dive into the river to retrieve things from Lewis and Clark's capsized boats. How I wish I could have given her a ride around the hard parts of her river journey.

Paul McCartney's Inspiration: Katrina

This entry is more about spontaneous fun than accessibility. Carrie and I learned that my two Beatle-crazed sons, Samuel and Ben, were going to a Paul McCartney concert in Vancouver, Canada as a welcoming party for Samuel (on the left) who had just moved to the Northwest. It didn't take Carrie long to jump on the idea to go with them. The Beatles are the most important musical group to Samuel. They shaped most of his childhood and adolescence being a big part of his relationship with his dad. Turned out selecting accessible seats in the coliseum required puzzling a maze of numbers, but we got the tickets! The seats gave us a great view. Watching Carrie sing along with Paul McCartney, I was grateful to the guys for letting us tag along.

Paul McCartney's Inspiration: Carrie

Yes, I did sing with Paul Mccartney that night. And my voice came from deep inside my heart when he asked us all to scream at once to recreate the early Beatles days Does anyone remember that?

I left inspired by what Paul McCartney is still creating and giving. The concert lasted two and a half hours without a break. At age 77, Paul McCartney was the lead singer on every song, played six different instruments multiple times, and entertained us between each song with first-hand Beatles' stories. I left willing to drop that I'm old at age 63. No, I have lots more to do.

AGUA PURA CATALINA

July 2019: Guatemala

Kayaking at Hotel Atitlan with Rudy: Katrina

Calm, Katrina, Calm!" was the mantra this young man would say as he smiled back at me through the rear view mirror of his uncle's truck while deftly driving the tight curves of Guatemala, so reminiscent of the Amalfi Coast in Italy. Rudy was our wheels and one of our guides, and most important, Carrie's devoted Guatemalan assistant. Upon greeting, he immediately took her chair from my hands. We simply would not have made it around Guatemala without Rudy. This generous and sensitive young man brought extra joy to my adventure. The two of us laughed and shared a great deal with the help of our Google Translators. Carrie knew Rudy from sponsoring him as a child in a program for children in Guatemala whose families needed financial help.

Kayaking at Hotel Atitlan with Rudy: Carrie

We found out our hotel on Lake Atitlan had small plastic kayaks to use--woo,hoo. But, before getting too jazzed, I always need to ask "Is there an accessible way to the water?" They said no, there's a very steep ramp and lots of cement stairs. But, between me and my two able attendants (Katrina and Rudy), we made a way. The accessibility tip this time featured life vests used as knee pads. Adults don't have fat pads on their knees like babies. So when we crawl on a roof or in my case to get down stairs, padding for the knees is essential. To get to the lake this time, we took off our life vests which provided nice, thick padding for my knee.

When we finally found ourselves on the water in kayaks, we were shining as bright as the sun on the lake.

Hotel Atitlan Gardens: Katrina

After lunch and a common rain shower, we would stroll through the beautiful gardens that we found outside our door. Carrie's wheelchair fit easily down every grass or stone pathway at the Lake Atitlan Resort, in Panajachel, Guatemala. I marveled that there were endless gardens to discover, everyday a new rose, or cacti, passion flowers, and several colorful talking parrots. I learned that people flew in by helicopter just to have lunch among the gardens here at the resort. Our daily adventures reminded me of what it might be like to walk through a Beatrix Potter storybook or to be a young Mary Lennox discovering a Secret Garden.

Hotel Atitlan Gardens: Carrie

A nod to Katrina's Secret Beatrix Potter Garden of giant cacti. I have one of these succulents in a three inch pot at home; it's tiny. The same plant in Guatemala is bigger than I am.

Leaving Katrina to her botany, my hotel hang-out was this jacuzzi with water that looked like it was tumbling over a cliff. I could enter here easily from my wheelchair and be in one of the most beautiful places on earth.

This is also where the helicopters bringing lunch guests to our hotel would land. I felt some envy; helicoptering seems a luxurious way to travel, avoiding the congested roads we traveled to get here. But then, we aren't Drug Lords (called narcotraficantes in Guatemala). The Drug Lords are the rich and powerful in Guatemala; and I suspect some of them are the ones who fly around in helicopters. The drug lords terrorize the humble Guatemala people which is a major reason why Guatemalans leave their homeland and make the long, dangerous journey to the US. Escaping the Drug Lords, and abject poverty, is the only future they see for their families.

Journey to Santa Catarina Palopo, Lake Atitlan: Katrina

The local rooster greeted us as we passed water gushing out of pipes onto our path. My favorite adventure in Guatemala was the trek to the home of a Mayan family we met during our second day at Lake Atitlan. A mother and father inspired us to visit their home where they lived with their five children and grandmother. They were from nearby Santa Catarina, a lake town painted with 100 gallons of turquoise enamel to celebrate a village of generational weavers such as the women in this family. They were eager that I experience their Temazcal, a Mayan sauna with healing rituals passed down through generations like their weaving symbols. While I sat in a pew at the Santa Catarina Cathedral learning about Mayan traditions from the mother through Google Translator, the father slipped away to start the fire in the sauna. When he returned the father and Rudy deftly wheeled Carrie up steep and slippery sidewalks to their home. Inside, Carrie was handed a smiling baby from a hammock and I was dressed in a traditional Mayan huipil (we-peel) blouse and headdress. Before descending the hill, I took in the view of the tin red rooftops below and all the various signs of life in each home. I so enjoyed the family'shospitality and hold a deeper understanding that their daily survival is primarily dependent on sharing their culture with strangers.

Journey to Santa Catarina Palopo, Lake Atitlan: Carrie

The steep walk up to the Mayan family's house in a deluge of rain may be my most bona fide adventure yet. The rains, which typically begin in May, hadn't even started in many areas when we arrived in July. The spigot was opened during our trek up to see the family's house and hand-made Mayan weavings. So up we went through this bumpy composite cement and mud alley with its stony stairs, narrow but colorful passages, and ankle-spraining ruts in a drought-breaking downpour. A challenge for everyone--the men huffing and puffing to transport the wheelchair, Katrina keeping the camera dry enough to take pictures, someone to clear the chickens from the path, and admittedly, yours truly on the wheelchair. I don't think GPS would have known where to send us, but a family member led the way to the house that has been in the family for generations. I apologized afterward to the father of the family for putting him through this. He responded with a big "no problema" and said that I wasn't the first wheelchair to go up this alley. An example of the "can-do" Guatemalan character.

Monkeying Around at the Reserva Natural Atitlan: Katrina

While kayaking in Lake Atitlan we heard a zing above our heads, and then spotted people soaring down a zipline at an incredible height and speed along the mountain side. Bucket list. However, after exploring the trail to the zipline, I learned the route to the lines would be inaccessible, riddled with rocks and mud from recent rains. The park suggested the easily accessible butterfly house for Carrie. We inquired, what about the monkeys? The attendant winced. Probably not. That trail was also challenging with multiple stairways and boulders. The three of us knew we could tackle the trail. Determined with a willingness to explore the upper forest canopy where the spider monkeys welcomed bananas, we pressed on with Carrie on her knees, Rudy carrying the wheelchair and me documenting our determined tenacity with photos.

Monkeying Around at the Reserva Natural Atitlan: Carrie

Looking at these photos shot by Katrina we do seem like a well-orchestrated hiking group, gaining an impressive amount of elevation on this jungle trek. Katrina climbs high and gets birds (or monkey) eye view photos. Speaking of Katrina's photos, we have precious extra-sharp photos of our adventures this year due to Katrina's artist eye and her well-chosen Pixel camera. What Katrina sees contrasts with my view of things when I'm going up the stone stairs on my knees. I see only the next step, six inches at a time hand, knee, hand, knee. A Zen-like mindfulness pace.

All in all, it was invigorating to be part of our crew which climbed to where we could share bananas with these lively monkeys in the wild. In fact, it almost made me thankful that I didn't qualify for ziplining that day.

AMIDI Water Project in PACHAY: Katrina

Rudy drove Carrie and me to a small village outside of Antigua, Guatemala where Ana Maria Chalí Calan and the women of Pachay bring sustainable living conditions to their village. At the base of the village road we picked up Ana Maria, the leader of AMIDI (Asociación de Mujeres Indígenas Para Desarrollo Integral: Association of Indigenous Women for Holistic Development). Rudy's truck pulled us up the winding rut and pot filled dirt roads to the tip top of the small village where we were warmly greeted by Ana Maria's daughters and other Mayan women and children from Pachay. The women were eager to speak with Carrie, to show her their fine building she had helped to sponsor. My favorite moment of our meeting was when two women plopped live rabbits and chickens on the table to illustrate their passion for their poultry business. The intelligence of Maria's daughters as they outlined their organic gardening methods was stunning to me. Just before the group photo, Carrie, a strong woman with the help of tough women, ascended the top of the building. After goodbyes, Ana Maria joined us on the ride back to the city where she intended to use the library to continue her research on advocacy for women's rights in Guatemala.

AMIDI Water Project in PACHAY: Carrie

A few years ago, I learned of this group of Mayan women from *Parade* magazine of all places. They were featured because they were using Mayan traditions to build better lives for their families now. In 2018, their project was to bring water to their town for the first time ever. They had negotiated to purchase a spring up the mountain to provide water, they had a design with budget figures for a cistern and even ... bathrooms! We went to see their water system now finished. A big part of the project was the cistern which opened on top of this building. I asked to see it also. It took a village to help me up the steep muddy path across the plank in my wheelchair, up the ladder, and finally getting pulled up to the roof. I can see that the "can do" spirit of the AMIDI women will carry them far.

Visiting Transitions Foundation: Katrina

I would have stayed in Guatemala in a heartbeat to work for Transitions, the foundation co-founded by Alex Galvez. Alex explained to me that he was shot in Guatemala City when he was 15 years old. He was walking to a grocery store when a gang member aimed a gun at his head. Alex dodged that bullet, but the second went in his shoulder and out the other, severing his spinal cord in its path. Alex was found by American John Bell in a hospital sick from bed ulcers. John took him to Washington DC, where Alex recovered after two years, returning with John to co-found Transitions. Alex, now the executive director, manages several programs. The foundation has a factory making wheelchairs proudly run by Guatemalan citizens. For many years they have had an athletic program with a highly competitive basketball team. They also provide a teacher and facilities for a special needs classroom in San Antonio Aguas Calientes outside of Antigua.

Transitions is one of two organizations that will benefit from sales of this book.

Visiting Transitions Foundation: Carrie

Alex and the other wheelchair users at Transitions bravely face daily mobility challenges. Guatemala doesn't provide the type of social services offered in the U.S. and many adults, as well as children, are isolated at home if they can't walk. A wheelchair can make a great difference in opening up a life. Not only does Transitions improve lives through matching people in need with wheelchairs, it also employs mostly wheelchair users in its factory. And for fun? These guys are tenacious on the court playing wheelchair basketball with their jazzy sports wheelchairs. The Transitions team is the best in Guatemala and they also play in international tournaments with Mexico, Canada, and other countries.

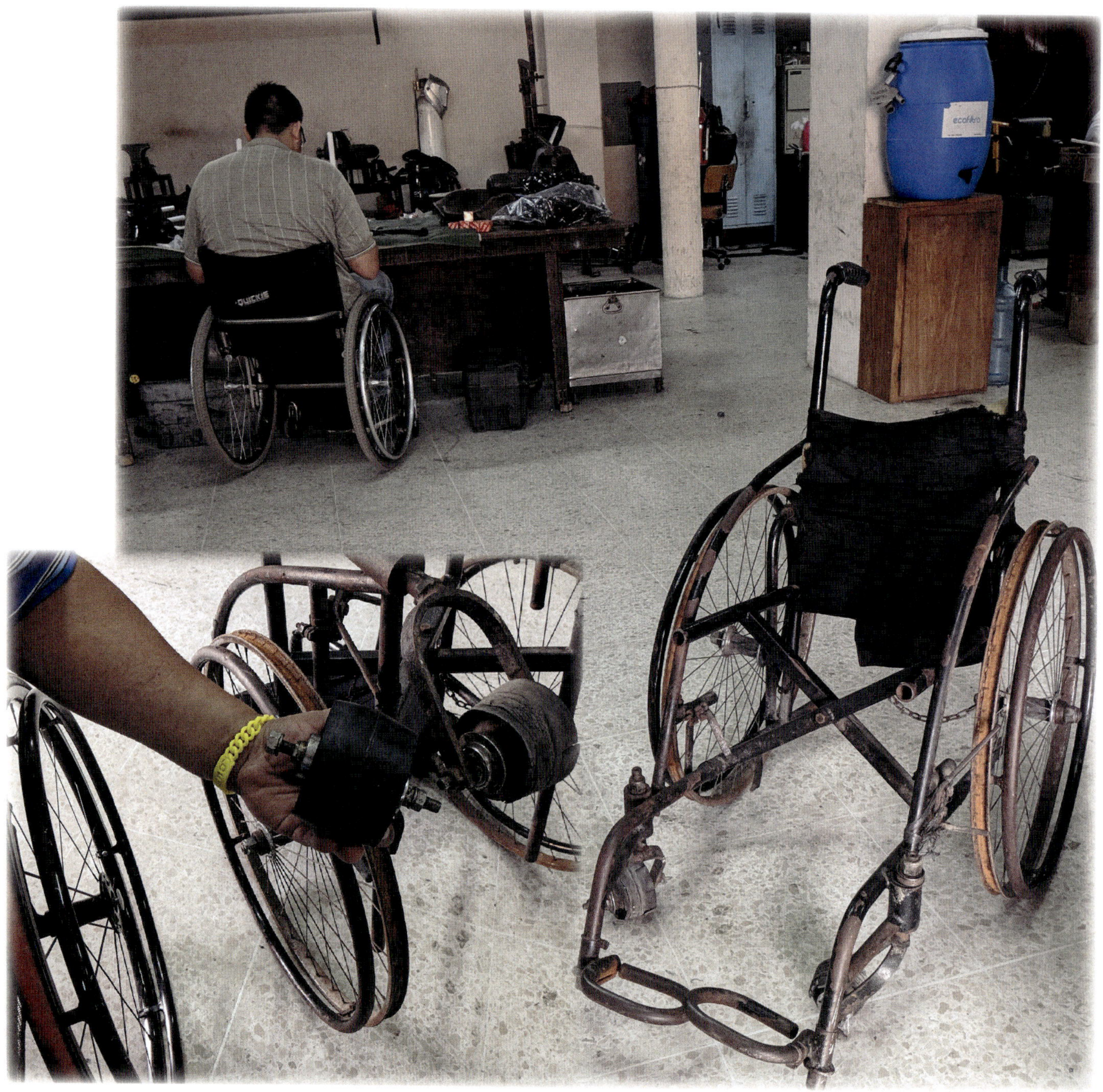

Carrie gets a new wheelchair: Katrina

I pondered the rusty wheelchair with Alex. We agreed it had probably been owned by a homeless man. I think I understood correctly that Transition's wheelchair factory will replace the parts of any of their returned factory made wheelchairs, such as the worn wheels on this one. The chair was one of the factory's originals. Alex mused that they might just replace the chair with a new lighter aluminum version. The factory's goal is to make 300-500 chairs a year. Carrie began asking questions about models. I noticed that each of the men working at Transitions had a unique wheelchair to fit their body size and preference of wheels. Carrie hopped on one of the floor models. The men cautioned her not to tip back on the lighter weight chairs. She wondered if this is why they could jump up curbs and over obstacles. They said they can "only" go up four inches and that it's mostly dexterity and skill, but it can help to have the right chair.

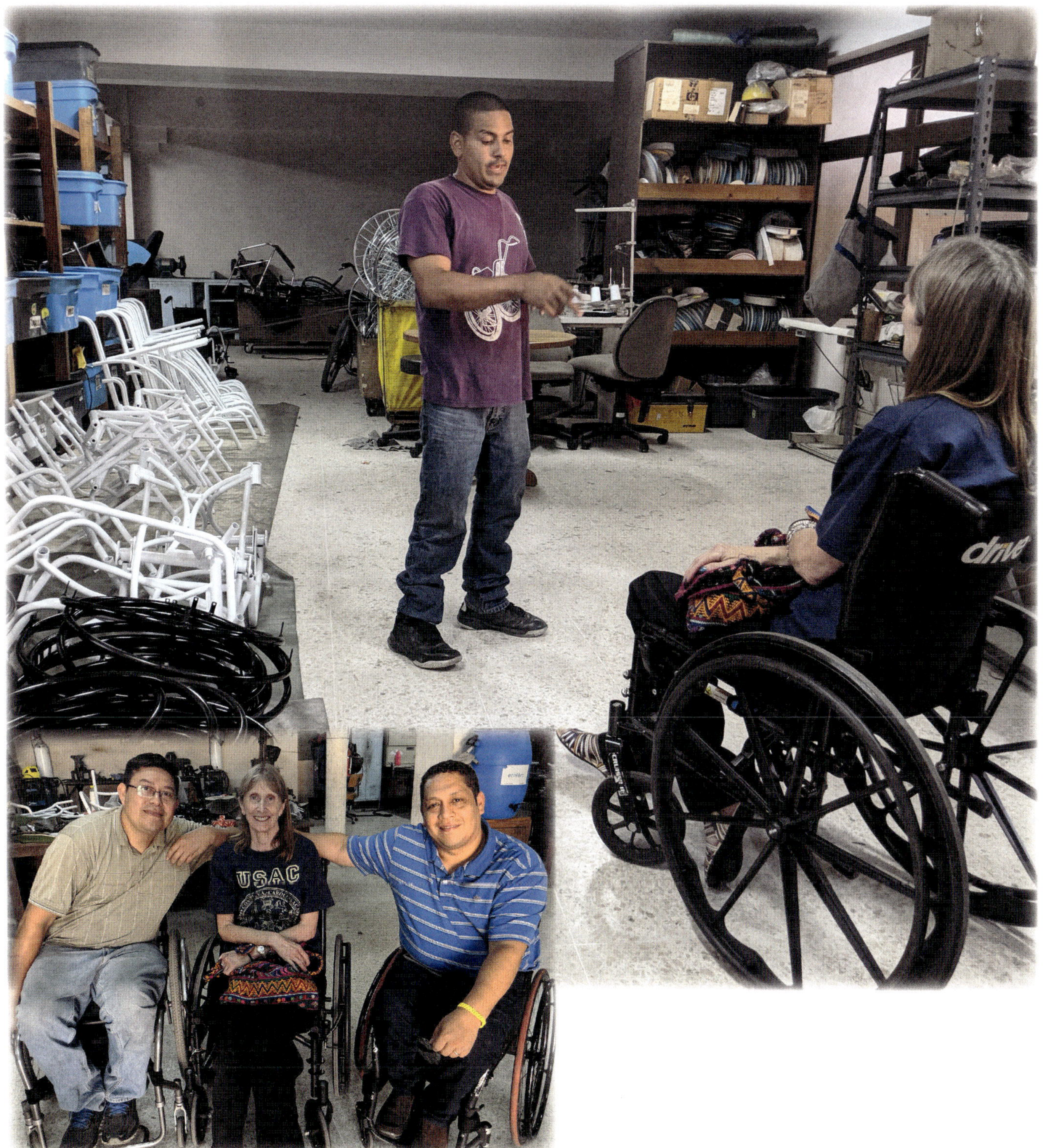

Carrie gets a new wheelchair: Carrie

I own a couple of wheelchairs that are relatively small and light at 25 pounds. I think I'm quite adventurous with these wheelchairs. But Hugo (purple t-shirt) at Transitions looked at my wheelchair and put it in the "hospital wheelchair" category. That set me back, so I started asking about getting a sportier wheelchair. They took my measurements, and asked a couple of questions like "would I like brakes?" The hitch? They need me to travel back to Guatemala to pick it up. "Okay." I smiled.

San Antonio Aguas Calientes: Katrina

Alex seemed to know everyone. For example, collecting Carrie and me from our hotel, he drove us through Antigua's town square stopping to casually converse with a local supporter. Transitions is always looking for financial contributions for their projects which includes a special needs classroom outside of Antigua. The students we met had a variety of physical disabilities. I learned attendance is challenging because families tend to keep their children home to work for them. Transitions attempts to educate the parents as well as the community on the importance of an inclusive education.

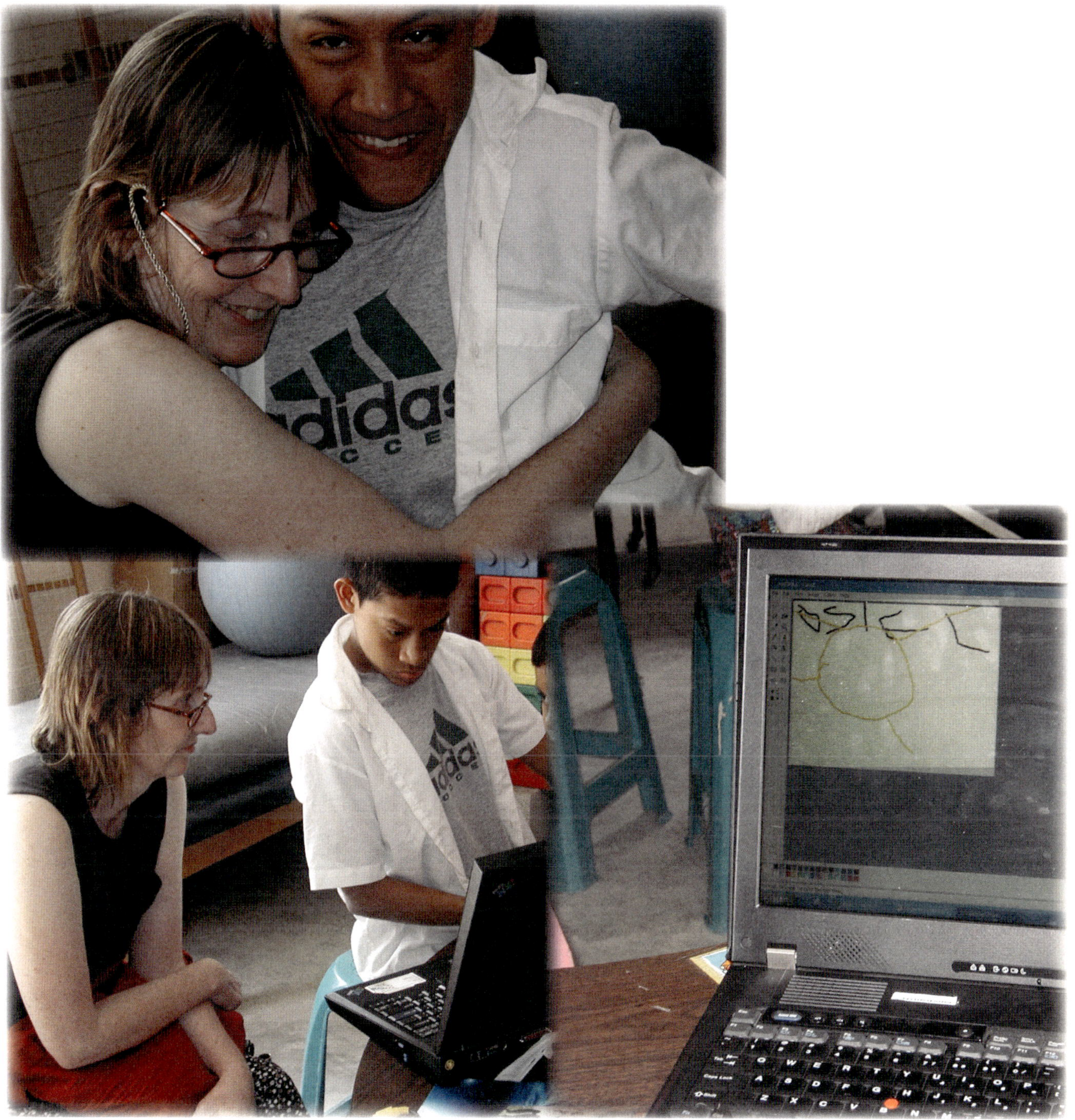

San Antonio Aguas Calientes: Carrie

My story with Transitions' special needs school began sixteen years ago. I came across their website, liked a mission for kids and wheelchairs in Guatemala, and offered my support. They asked that I sponsor a student at their special needs school, Osiel. As I understand, Transitions found Osiel, age twelve, when he had been pretty much confined to his bed at home because he couldn't walk. Transitions provided a wheelchair and Osiel began attending their special needs school. After a year of sponsoring Osiel, I traveled to the school to meet him and take him a laptop I had been using. That was a popular thing to do—all the students loved the computer, but especially Osiel. I was impressed that he immediately wrote his name so I could see it on the screen. Big hugs all around. I didn't go to Guatemala for many years and lost touch with Osiel.

Osiel: Katrina

It was inspiring to meet Osiel and witness what had become of Carrie's gift to that teenager many years ago. Osiel is now 30 years old and though he is not able to communicate with spoken words, he operates his own innovative internet cafe in the small village of San Antonio Aguas Calientes outside of Antigua. Rudy, who was also with us, brought my attention to a sign in the cafe that translates in English: I am Osiel the owner of the internet. If you have patience, it will be my pleasure to assist you. Any questions about computers ask without embarrassment. When I lower my head is YES. There is a short documentary film about Osiel made in 2017. On Youtube: "Osiel Martinez Internet Cafe Guatemala 2017"

Osiel: Carrie

I learned about a year before that Osiel had an internet cafe and happily started sending funds for his business But, given how severe I remembered his disability, I couldn't quite feature Osiel's having an internet cafe. I was eager to see Osiel and his café on this visit so after seeing the school, we went to his business. There was Osiel, same contagious grin, but now 30 years old. I was very moved because although I still couldn't understand him, he was obviously a very accomplished young man. This brave guy, who can't talk nor control his very awkward movements, founded an internet cafe. Now that's a "differently enabled" triumph. No question why mom is smiling. On Youtube: "Osiel Martinez Internet Cafe Guatemala 2017"

The Infamous Cobblestones of Antigua: Katrina

Carrie had warned me all year, when we were clunking through Rome, and weaving through DC's older streets, that I hadn't seen anything until I experienced the cobblestones of Antigua, Guatemala. We arrived at night bumping along in the truck to loud music, lights and crowds of people in the town square. In the days that followed, I walked the stone roads in the early mornings. I became fixated on the textured cobblestone street structure, and haunted by the question of accessibility. I began to keep a photo journal of the tiled markers throughout the old city. I was perplexed that the city deemed the crumbling sidewalks and cobbled streets accessible. Curiously, I didn't notice any other wheelchair users. And why in this modern age did cars bounce over streets in the oldest city of Central America? When I asked our local guide, he said the city council intentionally chose to keep the cobblestone to deter the fast pace of the much more modern and often violent Guatemala City. I prided myself in assisting Carrie over these stones without calling a local Tuk Tuk. With the help of Rudy and our trusty tour guide Hugo, Carrie was able to play in the street life with us.

The Infamous Cobblestones of Antigua: Carrie

Yes, I want it all, don't leave me home when you go out, please. Rudy, whom you've already met, turned rickshaw driver in the colonial city of Antigua. Rudy is endlessly patient. I heard only "where next" as I led him on an hour-long wild goose chase. I just hope Rudy could stand up straight again after we left.

If it weren't for Antigua's cobblestones. we might never have met Hugo. Our first morning in Antigua, Katrina and I headed out to its main square. The curbs there can be an intimidating two feet above the street. A kind man saw us and came over to help Katrina lift me up. On the way back, he helped again. We found out this was Hugo Gutierrez, a tour guide, and we were blessed with his company during all the rest of our Antigua stay.

August 2019:

Summer Floats and Kayaking

Wenatchee River Float, WA: Katrina

Upon returning from Guatemala Carrie and I continued our exploration of rivers with the wild Wenatchee in Leavenworth, Washington. We were scheduled to go on an easy float with Osprey, our trusted whitewater company, but they claimed there was absolutely no accessibility for a wheelchair because of rocks and steep banks. Their hands were legally tied. Ever persistent, we found a local access point. The company let us use their tubes. It was not as rocky and steep, and there were two nice men to help maneuver Carrie's chair safely to the water.

Wenatchee River Float, WA: Carrie

My expeditions this year consistently seem to have "two nice men" to help. It makes for a friendly universe. I'm here also with long-time friend Nadine Sanders. She's been with me on many trips including Guatemala and Mexico. Maybe more importantly, we've supported each other over many years to manifest the experiences and adventures we feel nudged to do. Tubing the Wenatchee River for example.

Skookumchuck Bounce House and Other Forms of Accessibility: Katrina

The goal was to float local rivers in Washington and Oregon in the warm summer months. We learned of many methods to maneuver to and from the water. The inner tubes became a vehicle for accessibility. Carrie discovered they were also perfect for crawling out of the river over long paths or in tight spots. It was when riding down the Skookumchuck River that Carrie got the idea to jump from a rope swing into a tube. I also witnessed Carrie's versatility, like when she used her flip flops for paddles to push water, and her knee pads to cross river banks.

Skookumchuck Bounce House and Other Forms of Accessibility: Carrie

Oh joy, truly a summer on the river, including many floats on the Skookumchuck and Chehalis rivers in my own hometown. I'm chuckling in this photo because it's my first time floating under this bridge, a bridge that I crossed over a few thousand times as a child in the family car.

Once on these rivers, I can paddle and steer like anyone. But the "once on the river" is the rub. Getting from the car into the river at various times has involved the following for my helpers. Rolling the chair on rocks, mud and sand. Getting scratched going through blackberry brambles. Steep uphills and steep downhills lugging floaties. Giving me piggyback rides, dragging me by one arm and carrying me in a two person shoulder seat. Someone then has to make the long trek back to store my wheelchair in the parked vehicle. For my helpers, this all gets repeated on the other end of the float.

Whidbey Island Kayaking in Langley, WA: Katrina

I simply love the marks wheels make in the sand. I have a photo album of twirls and circles and deep cut lines like these. It is never easy getting a wheelchair to the beach. The rewards of reaching the water are worth the effort. We joined a tour of kayakers on the Saratoga Passage. Once on the water, we found ourselves restless to go farther than the large group. With the help of our seaesoned guide Tabitha, we learned new strokes to go FASTER! We liked to push our adventures, even in the water.

Whidbey Island Kayaking in Langley, WA: Carrie

It still surprises me each time I see a picture of myself in a wheelchair. Like, “What’s a lady in a wheelchair doing going kayaking?” Oh, that’s me.

Everyone at Whidbey Island Kayaking was kind and made sure I could go kayaking. Mostly they get on board after they see that I have someone, i.e. Katrina, who is majorly responsible for me. The kayak guides understandably like to have an able-bodied companion. And so do I. Katrina can always paddle when I get tired, navigate the way back, or drag me across sand, allowing for an edgier kayaking trip than it would be based on only my abilities.

We kayaked perhaps more than any other water adventure this year, in places as varied as Cancun in Mexico, Lake Atitlán in Guatemala, and the Salish Sea here in Washington state.

Bowman Bay Kayaking, WA: Katrina

The textured ramp gave Carrie access to what we agreed was our most rugged kayaking adventure to date. Once in the water, Carrie paddled in front as the power, and I managed our course with a rudder in the back. We were skeptical whether we would enjoy kayaking in the morning fog. We signed up with Anacortes Kayak Tours for a two hour trip on Bowman Bay in the Deception Pass State Park of Whidbey Island. It was our first time at this Bay, so we didn't know what sweet sights lay ahead of us. The fog guided my gaze to the skin of water we were on. Salty waves rolled under our kayak as large swells. Our guide, Max, explained the swells were from storms that had once been active in the Pacific ocean beyond the Salish Sea.

Bowman Bay Kayaking, WA: Carrie

Driving up to Anacortes Kayak Tours that morning was sobering. We had kayaked the day before in bright sunlight among lots of buildings and surrounded by more than a dozen other kayakers. What we saw here was dense fog, nothing manmade and we were alone. Shall we go through with it? Before I could back out, our guide appeared, looked us over and apparently deemed us seaworthy. We were committed. First up in "real" kayaking was a new apparel item, cockpit skirts. So far, so good. Second consequential difference is that we needed both a power person and a steering person. (Katrina had done both before). Steering involves feet and so had to be Katrina. That put me as power person-yikes. Once we put in, we were in a glorious world of rough ocean, fog and wilderness. It was enchanting. Our guide must have thought he had good material in his clients because he offered to give us the fairly rare opportunity to go near a cave that couldn't be accessed any other way. The risk? Get too close and get sucked inside, which was Katrina's worry. Not mine, the guide had showed me how to paddle backwards and I was ready at the bow for any quick getaway. So glad we didn't bail and instead had a genuine kayak adventure.

Toutle River, WA, Rock Bed: Katrina

This photograph is of a woman who just experienced the thrill of a new sport. It wasn't floating the Toutle, it was crawling the very long expanse of hot boulders from the river to the trail at the edge of the forest, which she also climbed. After mapping out the access points her friends and I played "Marco, Polo" to be sure our aim from the river bed to the forest trail was on point. We thought Carrie would be carried most of the way from the river. She had other ideas, as usual!!!

Toutle River, WA, Rock Bed: Carrie

Coming out of the Toutle River after our float, there was a long bed of boulders to get to the car. These likely weren't unfamiliar rocks to me. Growing up, our family had property on the Toutle River near this very spot. Our fun river play ended when Mt. St. Helens erupted 40 years ago. Hot mud overflowed the bed of the Toutle leaving our land unrecognizable and almost no river. The river is finally back enough to make a float possible. But there is still much less water and these very rocks I'm going over no doubt formed the river bed in front of where our cabin had been. Count the ironies—over 50 years after we spent summers in our cabin on the Toutle River, i would be going over this same rock bed. And that 22 years after MS landed me on a wheelchair I'm still adequately enabled to traverse the rocks.

The Fast and Furious Willamette River in Albany, OR: Katrina

I became nervous when I saw the fast pace of the Willamette River. I had learned by now to be open to all possibilities, but I hesitated. The hesitation cost us time in the sun on a cold river in the late afternoon. We weren't from the area, and I saw no one floating except a passing kayak. I called out for advice. "Sorry, we can't stop!" they yelled back as they whooshed away. I asked some locals wading on the shore. They advised not floating on the river. I called the Visitor's Center. They weren't sure. Okay, but here we were. I took in a deep breath, or two, and then remembering the email from the man at the local Visitor's Center who had never floated on the river. He suggested getting in at Hyak Park and out at Bryant or Bowman. Bryant to Bowman looked really scary swift. I decided on Hyak to Bryant because it was the shortest float. Once at Hyak even Carrie paused. But we went in to the vast, huge, fast river. That night we saw Amy, the woman from the Visitor's Center I had consulted by phone. We crushed each other with hugs because we had lived!

The Fast and Furious Willamette River in Albany, OR: Carrie

We agreed on an outing to Albany. We would go to the balloon festival for Katrina, and go on a river float for me. When the river didn't look as easy as we thought, Katrina went into mode of, "I'm going to make this work for Carrie," which Katrina does, and she came through. We had a great float, definitely the swiftest river we had been on, no paddling needed.

We had no wheelchair at the end of our float on the Willamette, so I crawled on floaties all the long way from the river shore to the parking lot (with Katrina lugging one after another). There we discovered the Uber driver didn't show. A woman at the park offered to take us to Katrina's car. When we got there, I asked Katrina for my wheelchair. The woman from the park, who had seen me come all the way unaided from the river, protested "you don't need a wheelchair." I enjoyed being perceived as sturdy-bodied.

Visiting the Rolling Pilot at the Northwest Air and Art Festival in Albany, OR: Katrina

I thought of it. I thought of taking a picture of Michael's famous big grin as he reached out to hug Carrie, but I didn't. I wanted to be completely in the moment when Carrie extended her hand out to Michael's hug saying to him, "I've never had anyone work so hard to give me a hug." I had gone through the security tape to greet Michael and meet his balloon crew chief and fellow pilot. After warm greetings, and a pause in the conversation about preparation for the night's GLOW event, I asked if I could bring Carrie over to say hello. He offered to come to her instead, wheeling himself over the turf, and then apologizing to the spectators as he moved their blankets on the lawn so he could wheel towards Carrie. It had been eight months and many adventures since Lake Havasu City. I will always be grateful for this trail blazing man who got us started, and opened my eyes wider to the fun in the moment.

Visiting the Rolling Pilot at the Northwest Air and Art Festival in Albany, OR: Carrie

As noted earlier, Michael Glen is the pilot who has a special harness for wheelchair people to ride in. At this Albany event as he rolled over to greet me I had time to admire Michael's wheelchair skills. It's impressive that he always pushes his own chair himself. He has even taken the handles off the back of his chair so people absolutely can't push him!

With Michael present, I gave a plug for Katina to be on the balloon crew. "She would be a great addition to the balloon crew based on the adventure skills I've seen her use in action." He pointed to the lot where they would fly the next morning and said we were welcome to join them as we had done in Lake Havasu in January. I slept in while Katrina returned to the balloon festival and helped Michael's crew in the morning. No doubt to me which adventure Katrina liked this year.

Visiting the Rolling Pilot, Day Two: Katrina

Once we got the balloons up into the air, I declined the offer to follow the bees in the crew truck, choosing to take photos on foot. They were headed for the lake. I made it to the bridge joining a small group of adults and children. All eyes gazed after the two colorful bees flying towards the rising sun in a clear morning sky reflected in the still waters of the lake. Children's voices exclaimed in joy and adults gasped as two bees became four when Michael and the other balloon pilot skillfully tapped their baskets on the surface of the "mirror." Tears of appreciation filled my eyes in the observation that the labor of these pilots and their crew brought joy and awe to the child within me. In that moment on the bridge Michael's ability to fly his balloons reminded me of my desire to serve children, and the child within adults; how pursuing one's passion can bring magic into the world.

Michael Glen is the Rolling Pilot, one of the organizations that will benefit from sales of this book.

Visiting the Rolling Pilot, Day Two: Carrie

Katrinas enthusiasm came across as she posted photo after photo of the balloons all around her where we had been just the night before. We heard early on in our balloon watching that there are more photos of hot air balloons than any other sporting events. That rang true watching Katrina's stream of photos from Albany. After learning at the Lake Havasu balloon festival that wheelchair users can't go up in a balloon, I'll always be jazzed remembering that we found a balloon with a harness and amazingly, up we went.

Wild Waves SPLASH: Katrina

Carrie and I visited Wild Waves in Tacoma, Washington as the summer grew hotter. The park had several accessible rides that kept us splashing for hours. Carrie even crawled up the stairs to the top of the tube tunnels. Staff never asked questions as Carrie wheeled herself to the top of the water slide, and then shot down the tubes. Our favorite ride was the glider planes. Lying flat on our bellies we soared up and down through the air. With Carrie's Accessibility Pass we went twice in a row!

Wild Waves SPLASH: Carrie

We have experimented all summer looking for the nicest river to float. And in the end we found it here at Wild Waves. It's called the Konga Lazy River, which loops around and around its turquoise riverbed. From ground level, you slide into an empty floatie as it goes by. The water is temperate, and the current is satisfying. A complete surprise to find the most floatable river at our own nearby theme park, Wild Waves, just off the freeway in Fife. I see season tickets in our future.

"Wimps" No More!: Katrina

As the summer came to an end so did our time together. Today marked the last day of playing in a river. We met Carrie's goal to rope swing in her childhood Skookumchuck. Carrie carefully assessed the river and the length of rope. I suggested we watch a couple of the kids who came by to swing. We observed their body soar as they tucked their legs and then dropped with a splash. With each of our attempts, we learned it takes a lot of upper body strength to soar and tuck in order to rope swing. Carrie crawled to the bank and got up on her knees grabbing the rope to swing out over the water, then again, and several more times, getting stronger and farther with each swing. We took turns, and afterward reflected that neither of us regularly chose to have similar fun like this when we were younger. And we wondered, as we come to a close, how are we going to take this awareness of risk and new adventure into other parts of our lives?

"Wimps" No More!: Carrie

I commented to Katrina that we should end our escapades with a big splash. And so we did. Dropping off the rope swing into the Skookumchuck River was the most adventurous splash I've ever made. And, yes, with that letting go of the rope over mid-river, something heretofore in my life I wouldn't have even entertained, I've slayed my childhood moniker, "wimp." In my mind, I'm now a "wimp" no more. Hallelujah, Jesus!

USAC

Conclusions

Watergate Kochari Rice and Remake: Katrina

Carrie and I found a meal worth mentioning in the midst of our tales of accessibility. We were looking for a simple meal on the rooftop restaurant at the opulent Watergate Hotel in May. We found it! The topic of food is also about accessibility. For example, this was a meal that even Carrie with her ileostomy bag could eat! OH MY!! This dish was mouthwatering and so good we ordered it two nights in a row. Just rice, "yellow lentils," caramelized onions, tomato, sauteed lemon, and a dash of chili oil, and garlic. It all tasted so smooth on the tongue. YUMM!!!! Which do you think is the Watergate dish, and which do you want?

Watergate Kochari Rice and Remake: Carrie

Yes, the more beautiful dish came from Katrina's kitchen. We are on a stay-cation writing retreat at Katrina's house in Chehalis, Washington. I usually avoid visiting in people's houses because it's too hard to get around inside. But other than popping the wheelchair up three front steps, this house is roomy with wide doors and easy passages. And just a stone's throw from the Chehalis River! We can take our floaties to the river on breaks from writing. How do I get to the river with its steep banks and brambles? Not an issue. After a summer of river floating, we've got it licked.

Tools for the Road: Katrina

When Carrie pulled out her gloves or knee pads, I usually saw her up to something adventurous! I remember Carrie wearing the gloves after we witnessed balloon pilot, Michael Glen display his strength and independence as he pushed himself up a steep ramp in his handleless wheelchair out of a restaurant. Soon after we arrived home, the gloves Carrie had stored in mothballs years before appeared on her hands.

Tools for the Road: Carrie

Whew, eight months of physical adventure. Many roads, paths and hotel halls donning gloves and rolling my wheelchair. Over a hundred stairsteps on my behind. And knee pads which helped me crawl up zipline ladders, in and out of boats, and dash across pavement to carnival rides. Katrina exerted her share of pushing, lifting, driving, navigating, lugging, running, climbing, steering, carrying, and dragging. All (well, mostly all) in a happy spirit of adventure.

Deception Pass Nighttime Bioluminescence Kayaking Experience: Katrina

It was overcast and gray when we arrived for the kayak tour on Bowman Bayonce again. The advertised sunset over the bay seemed unlikely. Our guide, Alex, very calmly gave us a floating tour along the cliffs while we waited for nightfall. And then our group let out a gasp as we rounded a corner. The sky and water were lit turquoise and a changing sky of rose, orange, and purple met our eyes. Alex quietly gestured for our small group of kayaks to draw close together. Collectively, we gazed at the glowing sunset in silence. I imagined the sky were lit with fireworks celebrating our year of adventures, a new set of colors going off with each drop of the sun below the horizon.

When dark set in so that we couldn't see our faces, we discovered more fireworks below the surface of the waters. We spotted a patch of glittering fluorescent life in a bed of coral. Our oars became glowing sticks of magic as they swirled through the black water stimulating plants and small animal life to ignite their lights. I remember my excitement when we scooped up a fluorescent critter that not even Alex could identify. We were curious explorers to the last moment.

"Have you heard what Carrie and Katrina are doing now!?" It is something unusual, yet makes perfect sense if you know the two of them.

Deception Pass Nighttime Bioluminescence Kayaking Experience: Carrie

A sunset kayak trip was a perfect last adventure for our year. Seeing this photo, and really all the photos of our adventures, I see our Bible verse for the year announced and completed.

"The earth is the Lord's, and all it contains, the world, and those who dwell in it. For He has founded it upon the seas and established it upon the rivers."

After an extraordinary eight months of travel now I go back to an also rich Centralia life. To paraphrase some Buddha "before adventuring, you chop wood, and carry water. After adventuring, you chop wood and carry water."

Oh yes, and there is the book to craft ...

Afterword: Katrina

What we are doing now: Traveling with Carrie as an "Adventure Specialist" was an amazing opportunity not only to explore new places in the world, but also to embrace the parts of me that thrive in facing challenges that come with ever changing situations. In asking myself, "What now?" I remembered the practice of being flexible in the moment and the courage to act even when others are shaking their heads.

When our travels came to a close I didn't want to stop exploring these practices. I went on a quest of my own to the southwest in the fall to test some of the things I had learned about being in the moment. Magic happened on a daily basis as I continued to embody this theory. I met a complete stranger who invited me to spend a few days with her at her timeshare while introducing me to the landscape and labyrinths of Sedona. In our search for labyrinths, we happened upon a special balloon ascension at 5:30 in the morning! And then on to The Albuquerque International Balloon Fiesta where I randomly walked through a tent and learned some pilots still needed crew for the week. I found myself gleefully signing up to be on a balloon crew for two seasoned Canadian pilots. I was flying high.

Traveling with Carrie in Mexico and Central America informed a question I had been living about how to serve immigrant families as an expressive arts therapist on the boarder of the USA and Mexico. It was a year of gathering information. No one I spoke with knew of any programs. Then suddenly after our travels I began meeting others who had been asking and living a similar vision. Through my work on the board with the International Expressive Arts Therapy Association I learned of several Expressive Arts Therapists developing a program called Voces Arts and Healing to serve immigrants in shelters throughout Juarez. They were seeking counsel from First Aid Arts; a program I learned was right in my back yard in Seattle, Washington. Expressive Arts Therapists through First Aid Arts have been training individuals serving refugees for 10 years now on how to use the arts to heal psychological trauma due to sex trafficking and displacement. I trained with First Aid Arts just before the Covid-19 pandemic put our nations in quarantine.

With the stillness that came for many of us during the quarantine, I was grateful for the time to finish *Differently Enabled Adventures*. The vision and writing of this book was my way to thank Carrie and the people we met.

What now? It's time to take some risks of my own.

May 22, 2020

Afterword: Carrie

What we are doing now: I ended my last page in this book: "After an extraordinary eight months of travel now I go back to an also rich Centralia life." This expectation was prescient-- it has been a very rich Centralia life, with nature and gardens, celebrations with housemates Mirna and Fátima, Laura Ingalls Wilder activities, and the joyous process of crafting Differently Enabled Adventures. The blessings continue, in spite of the fact that MS pain has had me homebound for the last six months.

As I write this afterward in May 2020, the global corona-virus crisis has all but shut down adventure travel in the countries we visited, namely Italy, Mexico, and Guatemala. Between the facts that with this MS pain I'm not able even to go out for a car ride, and that the world of travel has been stopped by a global pandemic, I'm doubly grateful for the blessed timing of our trips last year.

Connecting through God's Money Foundation is what's next for me. It's always been true for me that any pot of money I have is God's money, and in response I've been forming a foundation over the past few years. I use God's Money to participate with over 20 different projects such as Transitions (page) and Bread for the World (page). I also do things with children and their families that I have sponsored in Guatemala, Mexico and the US such as Rudy (page). I operate in a way that is not just writing a check, but is creating a connection. In the Bible, 2 Corinth 9:12 says being generous helps meet needs, and also provokes an outpouring of gratitude to God, and that is my mission.

God's money projects are on the Facebook page, "Gods Money 2 Corinth 9:12". You'll recognize this inspiring photo of our visit to the Cristo Redentor in Italy (page) as the logo on the Facebook page. You don't even need to have a Facebook account to access the God's money page. I'd love to hear from and connect you with any of the projects that interest you. I post weekly, and if you "Like" the Facebook page you can see new shares as they are added.

May 17, 2020

Appendix

It can be challenging and tedious to find the hotels and tours that offer accessible options. These individuals and organizations met us and exceeded our expectations.

JANUARY:

Tennessee

Gray Bear Lodge: Holistic Retreat Center
Address: P.O. Box 682, Hohenwald, TN 38462
Website: https://graybear.org/
Phone: 615-782-0469

Arizona

Lake Havasu City

Havasu Balloon Festival and Fair
Website: https://havasuballoonfest.com/

The Rolling Pilot
Michael Glen
Email: mglen42@rollingpilot.com
Website: www.rollingpilot.com
Cell: 520-349-4825

Nevada

Las Vegas

Rio Casio Zipline:
https://www.riozipline.com/

February

Cancun, Mexico

Amazing Adventure Park Cancun (ziplines and more)
website: https://atvamazingcancun.com/
Phone: +52 1 (998) 232 8443

Jungle Tour Barracuda

Website: https://jungletourbarracuda.com/
Address: Marina Puerto Madero. Blvd.
Kukulcán Km. 14.1 Cancun Hotel
Zone Q. Roo, 77500, Mexico
Phone: +52 (998) 88 52 444

Eco-Park Kantun Chi: Ecological Park of Caves and Cenotes

Website: https://www.kantunchi.com/en/
Address: Carretera Federal Cancún-Tulum, km
1266.8, Puerto Aventuras, 77734
Playa del Carmen, Q.R., México
Phone: +52 (984) 803 0143 +52 (984) 147 0280

Grand Royal Lagoon Hotel

Website: http://grandroyallagooncancun.com/
Address: Blvd. Kukulcan Km 7.5, Zona Hotelera,
77500 Cancún, Q.R., Mexico
Phone: +011 52 998 883 2749

Parasail Cancun

Website: https://www.parasailcancun.com/
Phone: +52 998 234 0872

Taxi we recommend in Cancun:
José Luis Reyna p.

Taxi: 7115
Phone: +1998 1807849
Email: Josetours@hotmail.com
Cancun Qroo Mexico

MARCH

Mazatlán, Mexico

Hotel Playa Mazatlán

Website: https://www.hotelplayamazatlan.com/
Address: 202 Playa Gaviotas Av., Golden Zone.
Mazatlán, Sinaloa, Mexico 82110
Phone: 52 (669) 9890555

Mazatlán Tours Aqua Sports Parasailing

Email: reservations@mazatlantours.org
Phone: USA/Canada: 1 (866) 471-4157/
International: +52 (669) 259-0211

APRIL:

Rick Steves' Europe, Inc.
Address: 130 4th Ave N, Edmonds, WA 98020-3114 USA
Phone: 425 771 8303
Email: rick@ricksteves.com

Italy

Dario Davide Archeologist, Historian, Tour Guide
E-Mail: dariodavide@virgilio.it
Web: www.dariodavide.com
Phone: 335/1041735

Accessible Tours:

On Sundays we arrange for free private tours in Pompeii for disabled visitors and their families. We understand that some people with disabilities do not have enough money to buy a private tour with an archaeologist because it is too expensive and it is difficult for them to organize their tours with other people because they have other needs. But Art must be for everyone. For this reason, every Sundays I organize a two-hour tour led by me to Pompeii for free. They fill the form and they reserve without spending anything for the tour—only for the entrance fee.

"Paint for Fun" thru Viator tours in Rome
Website: https://www.viator.com/tours/Rome/Paint-for-fun/d511-10338P10
Rome Tours with Rossana Lanucara, Tour Guide
Website: www.romeitalyexplora.com
Email: infor@romeitalycxplroa.com
Phone: +39 388 8621394 or +39 392 1462691

Grand Hotel Pianetamaratea Resort (near the Cristo Redentor)
Website: https://www.grandhotelmaratea.it/
Address: Contrada Santa Caterina, 50, 85046 Maratea PZ, Italy
Phone: +39 0973 871966

MAY

Washington DC

Boating in DC at the Key Bridge Boathouse
Address: 3500 Water St NW, Washington, DC 20007
Phone: (202) 337-9642

The Wharf Port of Anacortes in Washington DC now features an accessible riverfront with swings.

The Watergate Hotel
Website: https://www.thewatergatehotel.com/
Address: 2650 Virginia Ave NW, Washington, DC 20037
Phone: (844) 617-1972

JUNE

Washington State

Osprey Rafting Company

Website: https://ospreyrafting.com/
Address: 9342 Icicle Rd, Leavenworth, WA 98826
Phone: (509) 548-6800

World Kite Museum & Hall-Fame

Website: http://worldkitemuseum.com/
Address: 303 SW Sid Snyder Dr, Long Beach, WA 98631
Phone: (360) 642-4020

Beach Wheelchair avaiable here:

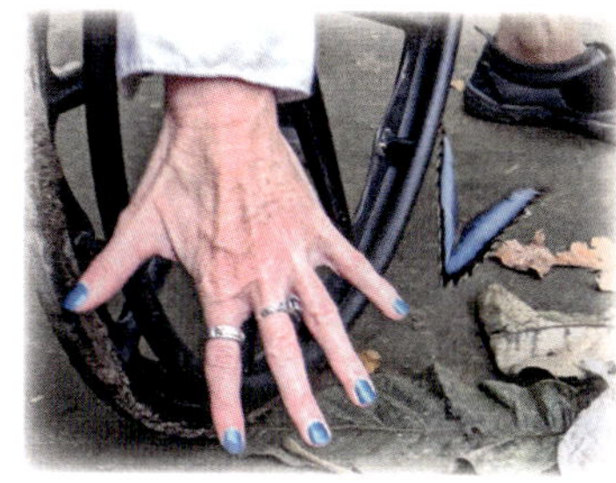

JULY

Guatemala

AMIDI Guatemala: Mayan Women Who Farm and Weave

Website: http://www.amidiguatemala.org/amidi.html
Email: info@amidiguatemala.org

Hotel Atitlán

Address: Finca San Buenaventura,
Panajachel, Solola, 07010 Guatemala
Website: https://www.hotelatitlan.com/
Phone: +502 79620404

Hugo Gutierrez, Travel Consultant

Antigua Guatemala
Email: hugobuenatierra@hotmail.com
Phone: (502) 4706 4832

Reserva Natural Atitlan (mariposa, monkeys, and ziplines)

Website: https://www.atitlanreserva.com/
Address: Antigua Finca San Buenaventura,
Panajachel 07010, Guatemala
Phone: 502 7762 2565

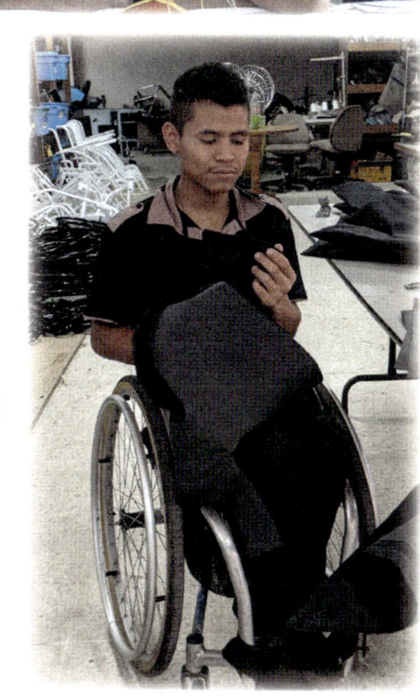

Transitions Foundation of Guatemala

Website: https://transitionsfoundation.org/
Friends of Transitions Guatemala is a US 501c3 organization EIN for FOTG is 83-1776455 based in 7 Overhill Rd Mill Valley CA 94941, whose mission is to provide support to Asociación Transiciones in Guatemala. Mobilizing Guatemalans with disabilities through rehabilitation, education, leadership skills, social integration and employment.

AUGUST:
Oregon

Northwest Air and Art Festival
Website: http://nwartandair.org/
Location: Timer Linn Memorial, Albany

Washington State

Anacortes Kayak Tours
Website: https://www.anacorteskayaktours.com/kayaking-day-trips/family-trips/
Address: 2009 Skyline Way, Anacortes, WA 98221
Phone: 360.588.1117 Or 800.992.1801

Whidbey Island Kayaking
Website: https://www.whidbeyislandkayaking.com/
Address: 201 Wharf St, Langley, WA 98260
Phone: (360) 221-0229

Wild Waves Theme and Water Park
Website: https://www.wildwaves.com/
Address: 36201 Enchanted Parkway S.
Federal Way, WA 98003
Email: Info@WildWaves.com
Phone: (253) 661-8000

Made in the USA
Coppell, TX
26 June 2020